AUSTIN FACES

of PHILANTHROPY

1976-2012

by **ROBERT GODWIN**

Waterloo Press
Austin History Center
PO Box 2287
Austin, Texas 78768-2287

First Edition
First Printing January 2013

ISBN 978-0-9888741-0-7

Printed in the United States of America
at OneTouchPoint-Ginny's Printing in Austin, Texas

TABLE OF CONTENTS

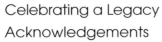

WHAT I LEARNED . . .

Before moving to Austin in 1961, D.J. and I were active in historic preservation and in contributing in various ways to our community. What we found on coming here was that the level of giving was downright pitiful. It cost $25 per couple (!) to attend the Symphony Jewel Ball, and $25 was about the normal gift amount, period; $100 was positively outstanding.

Mrs. Albert Jones, a friend of Ima Hogg, moved from Houston to a home near ours and was similarly dismayed. She called me one morning and said she would give $1000 to the symphony if D.J. would match it. He did. So did Ellen Garwood. And then Ronald Deford. At that time the only business in town that contributed was Southwestern Bell: they wrote a check for $500 the first of every year.

In 1972, I became president of the Austin Symphony (and held that post for 25 years), mostly because no man wanted the job and also, no doubt, because I was the only board member who had voted against declaring bankruptcy! We started contacting businesses. We contacted individuals. We always managed to have someone on the board who actually enjoyed doing this, and the rest of us followed suit. Unlike symphonies in other cities, we never sent out our executive director to ask for money; we, the volunteers, did that. We also started a phone-a-thon and quickly found that personal contact made all the difference. We never depended on state or federal grants. We showed ourselves to be fiscally responsible; our motto was, "You cannot be extravagant with other people's money."

And slowly over the years the level of giving rose and rose again. The Austin Symphony and so many other philanthropies proved themselves—largely by person-to-person contacts—to be organizations worth supporting. What seems to have stimulated both monetary contributions and volunteer hours in every instance was that someone you knew asked you to help. That knitted us all together and therein lay the vitality of the community.

People moving to Austin caught on, some more quickly than others, that it was important to participate, it was important to help, it was important to serve, and, yes, to contribute money. It felt good to give back.

It was good.
And it is good.

Jane Dunn Sibley
(Mrs. D. J. Sibley)

. . . AND WHY IT IS SO IMPORTANT

Opportunities for philanthropy and volunteerism whirl around us. This may be especially true here in Austin. Perhaps that is because, as a community, we have a culture of creating these opportunities and fulfilling them. Volunteerism has been a cornerstone of my life in Austin, beginning when I was a young housewife and new mother in the mid-1960's. I became active in the Austin/Travis County Mental Health Association, drawn to this organization both because my husband was a psychiatrist and because I had volunteered at the Austin State Hospital as a student at UT. Through my work in staging fundraisers and in finding donor prospects for the cause, I forged friendships with a diverse group of volunteers and staff, all of whom were devoted to improving the lives of the mentally ill. These bonds of friendship, formed through mutual values and time spent together, proved over and over again as enriching and as enjoyable as the knowledge and satisfaction of helping make the lives of those in need a little easier and more rewarding.

Philanthropy—the giving of oneself to others—is a gratifying practice. I have experienced enormous satifaction in initiating and participating in non-profit projects that have enriched all our lives in the areas of culture, literature, education, and social servies. My personal involvement has included restoration of the Paramount Theatre in downtown Austin, establishment of Philosopher's Rock in Zilker Park, formation of the Charles Moore Foundation for the Study of Place in West Austin, providing primary health care for the underserved at Peoples Community Clinic, founding and chairing (1996-2004) the Texas Book Festival, and founding the Molly Ivins Prize for Investigative Journalism to benefit *The Texas Observer*.

The success of these public and private projects has not been mine in isolation. But great joy and satisfaction have come from seeing needs met and horizons expanded and in developing wonderful, life-long relationships with my fellow citizens. There is a story that some 30 years ago someone wrote on a placemat in Sausalito, «Practice random kindness and senseless acts of beauty.» That's been happening in Austin, as documented in the photographic chronology of this book by Robert Godwin.

May the spirit of philanthropy continue and increase in this place we love, this City of Austin, Texas.

Mary Margaret Farabee
(Mrs. Ray Farabee)

All societies have exceptional qualities. They are embodied in exceptional people—people like Jane Sibley and Mary Margaret Farabee. Photography enables us to capture the lives of exceptional people and events at a point in time, allowing us to recall our past and create a context for the acts of future generations.

This book chronicles the spirit of community which has infused the life of Austin, Texas, with good works and cultural beauty. It is one of our strengths as a city, a city set on a hill that cannot be hid. The literally thousands of good causes that Austinites have advanced from the first days of our founding have enriched the lives of all who inhabit this lovely spot on the Colorado.

Acting together for the common good has created a spirit of community, an extraordinary vitality engendered by the sharing of talent, hours of service, and financial resources, that has made us a city dedicated to full participation of our citizens in the ongoing work of the betterment of life for all. We should all take great satisfaction from the long-standing involvement of our citizens, through their governmental, business, and the charitable (non-governmental) institutions in philanthropic efforts for the common good.

Through the lives of people like Jane and Mary Margaret and the thousand others depicted in this book, and following their good example, the spirit of community will surely live on in Austin, Texas.

Robert Godwin—in attending literally thousands of events, taking nearly a half million photographs, and caring so obviously about the good work in this community—has done the people of Austin an enormous service in providing this pictorial history of what makes us who we are.

Frank C. Cooksey
Mayor of Austin, Texas (1985-88)

When I began my photojournalism career, like most young news photographers, my focus was on "hard news"—fires, floods, wrecks and sports. These photos were the path to the ultimate goal of a Pulitzer Prize. Because I was working on a small daily, however, I had to shoot everything—features, ads and the dreaded "party pics" or "soc (social) shots." My formal attire consisted of a white no-press shirt and a pair of dark brown polyester pants from Sears. Scruffy was a kind adjective for my appearance.

After considerable tutelage, I came to understand the connection between the social world of Austin and the charity world of Austin. Supporting the Austin Symphony Orchestra pumped quality and life into the music, but it also supported the outreach programs which brought the Symphony into every Austin school. Who knows what that exposure to classical music inspired in the thousands of students present for those assemblies? That same ripple effect occurs in the other arts, social services and medical causes.

With **Austin Faces of Philanthropy**, I want to show not only the wide variety of philanthropic people but also those people maturing as they continue to serve. As they rolled through the decades, they drew new people to them who likewise drew new people. What was at best a meandering stream of a few hundred thousand donated dollars in 1976 is now a coursing river of tens of millions a year.

I hope that you, the reader, will take pride in what has been accomplished and encouragement for the work that lies ahead. Over the past four decades, I have observed service to the community be a family tradition—from parent to child, and now to grandchild. Even more, the "service to community" concept is contagious—passing from patron to client. As that client is helped, they go forward with the knowledge that as they have been helped, they need to do the same. That feeling becomes the thread that ties us all together as a city. Together we can continue to grow and offer greater opportunities for those following behind us.

I apologize in advance for mistakes and missing names. Being full of optimism, it is my hope to have an opportunity for a revised edition. Please send corrections and missing names to **aredub@earthlink.net**. Include the picture number and page number and know I will include it if a second edition becomes a reality.

Robert Godwin

CHAPTER ONE 1976–1981

During this period, the population of Travis County grew from 386,100 to 430,573. Dolph Briscoe was governor until Bill Clements took office in 1979. Jeff Friedman was mayor of Austin until Carol McClellan took over in 1977.

Major events of the time were Fiesta (benefiting the Austin Museum of Art at Laguna Gloria, Safari (benefiting the Natural Science Center) and Aqua Fest (benefiting all of Austin). Black-tie events included the Bachelors of Austin Presentation Ball, the Junior Helping Hand Home Gala, the Admirals Ball and the Jewel Ball (benefiting the Austin Symphony Orchestra).

Shooting this rodeo almost ended my career at an early point. I was shooting from inside the ring. When it was time for the bull riding, I would shoot the action, then watch the clowns and riders move the bull to the holding pen. Then I would get out my notebook for when the announcer was saying the rider's name. Did this for several riders, but as I was writing down a rider's name, I heard shouting and hoof beats at the same time. I looked up to see that a bull had escaped the riders and was headed right at me at full speed. In those days, I wore a rather battered straw cowboy hat and all I could think to do was snatch it off and swat at the bull's face while shouting "Go on!" Amazingly, the bull turned away and I discovered I had the power of levitation. Without any memory of jumping, climbing or flying, I found myself atop an eight foot fence—well away from any more bulls.

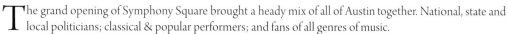

The grand opening of Symphony Square brought a heady mix of all of Austin together. National, state and local politicians; classical & popular performers; and fans of all genres of music.

1. Travis County Sheriff's Posse Rodeo 2. Grand Opening of Symphony Square 3. Frost Brothers fashion show for AAUW 4. Travis County Sheriff's Posse Rodeo 5. Willie Nelson at Symphony Square 6. Grand Opening of Symphony Square 7. Grand Opening of Symphony Square with Lloyd Doggett, Jane Sibley, Cong. Jake Pickle, Carol McClellan, & Peggy Brown 8. 1978 Admirals Club Queen Aliece Rowland escorted by Frank Morris, Jr. 9. Admirals Ball royal court 1978 Dana Painter, John S Joberg, Aliece Rowland, Christopher Heidrick, Mary Heidrick, Christopher Goldman

1

2

3

4

5

6

7

This was one of the early fashion shows for me—University Women's Club luncheon and show. It didn't sound too exciting and when I arrived at the event, it wasn't looking good. I was all of 24 years old and the event guests looked to be about a thousand years old on average. When the show started, however, I started fogging up my viewfinder at the vision of couture models in Albert Nipon lingerie. The crowd was decidedly appalled and sat on their hands—except to elbow their husbands who dared to applaud.

8

9

10

1. EBONY FASHION FAIR 2. CARLA BOOTH LEADS THE MODELS AT A CHRISTMAS AFFAIR 3. CON. JAKE PICKLE & MAYOR ROY BUTLER AT SYMPHONY SQUARE 4. EBONY FASHION FAIR 5. EBONY FASHION FAIR 6. SWIMSUITS IN WINTER AT JUNIOR LEAGUE A CHRISTMAS AFFAIR 7. AKIRA ENDO & CAROL MCCLELLAN 8-9. HATS & HISTORY 10. EBONY FASHION FAIR

1. Sue McBee   2. Hats & History for Heritage Society Alma Sioux Scarberry
3-4. Hats & History for Heritage Society   5. Ballet Austin Artistic Directors
Eugene Slavin & Alexandra Nadal   6. King Brio Will Wilson & family
7. Queen Christina Weeks dances with her father, Curtis Weeks   8. Hats &
History for Heritage Society   9. Dancers practicing for Nutcracker
10. Queen Christina Weeks

1. The Jewel Ball Royal Court in 1978   2. The 1978 Bachelors of Austin Presentation Ball was at the Driskill Hotel   3. The 1978 Bachelors of Austin debutantes   4. Morgan Hunter & Lucille O'Brien   5, 7, & 8. Big Brother Event
6. Paricia Morrison Fleming, Charles Morrison, friend, & Mary Lou Morison

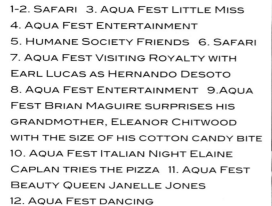

1-2. Safari   3. Aqua Fest Little Miss
4. Aqua Fest Entertainment
5. Humane Society Friends   6. Safari
7. Aqua Fest Visiting Royalty with
Earl Lucas as Hernando Desoto
8. Aqua Fest Entertainment   9. Aqua
Fest Brian Maguire surprises his
grandmother, Eleanor Chitwood
with the size of his cotton candy bite
10. Aqua Fest Italian Night Elaine
Caplan tries the pizza   11. Aqua Fest
Beauty Queen Janelle Jones
12. Aqua Fest dancing

1. VICTOR COSTA SHOW   2. CHRISTINA WEEKS MODELS VICTOR COSTA
3. HUMANE SOCIETY BENEFIT
4. CACTUS PRYOR & AMANDA BLAKE
5. VICTOR COSTA CROONS A TUNE
6. BETTY RAINEY MODELS VICTOR COSTA
7. AMANDA BLAKE MODELS IN HUMANE SOCIETY BENEFIT   8. CACTUS PRYOR MODELS FOR HUMANE SOCIETY
9. CHARLES BETTS   10. HUMANE SOCIETY STYLE SHOW   11. REALTORS WIVES CLUB
12. HUMANE SOCIETY APPEARANCE BY AQUA FEST QUEEN

1. Paramount Theatre   2. Frank & Tish Hall & Helen & George Covert
3. Heritage Society dance   4. Ernie May Miller   5. Tired volunteers,
Jennifer Moore & Laurie Hensley at the MDA Telethon   6. Lowell
Leberman with Carol McClellan   7. Dot Chaloupka announces a total
8. Bonnie & Clyde Smith   9. UT football coach Fred Akers with Mel
Pennington   10. Mel Pennington visits with Betty Himmelblau
during the MDA Telethon   11. Mel Pennington takes a moment of peace

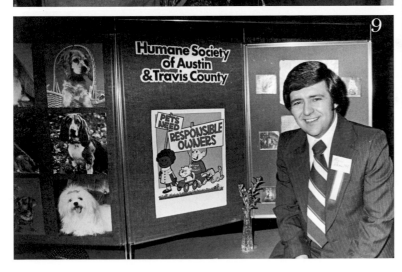

1. Austin notables working the phone bank at MDA Telethon 2. Dean Page Keeton 3. Dancing for Heritage Society
4. Heritage Society 5. Doyle Nordyke (Executive Director) & Marjorie Bird (Shelter Operations Director) dancing at Humane Society 6. Sport attire for Humane Society fashion show
7. Crowd for Humane Society 8. Fun Run at UT
9. Ben Prewitt visits Humane Society
10. Maurine & Willie Kocurek dance at the Folk Festival

1. Doyle Nordyke visits with fellow setting "doghouse sitting" record 2-3. Heritage Society 4. Austin Citizen editor Tom Reay arrives at the Caswell House for an event 5-6. Heritage Society 7. Heritage Society 8. Scholarship checks presented by the Civitans Club Heritage Society 9. Heritage Society

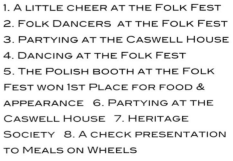

1. A LITTLE CHEER AT THE FOLK FEST
2. FOLK DANCERS AT THE FOLK FEST
3. PARTYING AT THE CASWELL HOUSE
4. DANCING AT THE FOLK FEST
5. THE POLISH BOOTH AT THE FOLK FEST WON 1ST PLACE FOR FOOD & APPEARANCE 6. PARTYING AT THE CASWELL HOUSE 7. HERITAGE SOCIETY 8. A CHECK PRESENTATION TO MEALS ON WHEELS

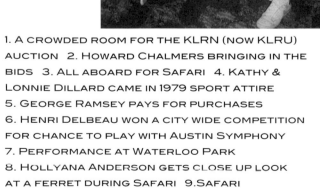

1. A crowded room for the KLRN (now KLRU) auction 2. Howard Chalmers bringing in the bids 3. All aboard for Safari 4. Kathy & Lonnie Dillard came in 1979 sport attire
5. George Ramsey pays for purchases
6. Henri Delbeau won a city wide competition for chance to play with Austin Symphony
7. Performance at Waterloo Park
8. Hollyana Anderson gets close up look at a ferret during Safari 9.Safari

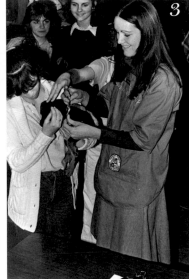

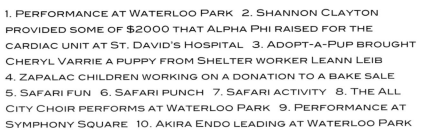

1. PERFORMANCE AT WATERLOO PARK 2. SHANNON CLAYTON
PROVIDED SOME OF $2000 THAT ALPHA PHI RAISED FOR THE
CARDIAC UNIT AT ST. DAVID'S HOSPITAL 3. ADOPT-A-PUP BROUGHT
CHERYL VARRIE A PUPPY FROM SHELTER WORKER LEANN LEIB
4. ZAPALAC CHILDREN WORKING ON A DONATION TO A BAKE SALE
5. SAFARI FUN 6. SAFARI PUNCH 7. SAFARI ACTIVITY 8. THE ALL
CITY CHOIR PERFORMS AT WATERLOO PARK 9. PERFORMANCE AT
SYMPHONY SQUARE 10. AKIRA ENDO LEADING AT WATERLOO PARK

1. WILLIE NELSON AT WATERLOO PARK   2. HOT DOG DINNER BENEFITING THE HUMANE SOCIETY
3. PERFORMANCE AT SYMPHONY SQUARE   4. A PAINTED FACE AT FIESTA   5. TURK PIPKIN PERFORMS
FOR THE CROWD AT FIESTA   6. PERFORMANCE AT SYMPHONY SQUARE   7. PROBABLY NOT LOST, BUT A
PLACE TO SIT AT FIESTA   8. LU ANN BARROW   9. GUSTAV LIKAN   10. BREAKING A CASCARONE ON
DAD'S HEAD AT FIESTA   11. FIESTA FUN WAS CASCARONES   12. CHILDREN'S ART AT FIESTA   13. SUSAN
WARREN CHAIRED THE ZACH SCOTT THEATRE COOKING SCHOOL BENEFIT   14. CAMILLE BENNET
STICKS TO HER POST AT SAFARI DESPITE THE RAIN

1. Carol Channing performs 2. Cactus Pryor & Lady Bird Johnson 3. Lady Bird Johnson & Carol Channing 4. Mayor Carole McClellan put to work 5. Charles Betts, Neal Spelce & John Hill at the opening of the renovated Tipps Building 6. Admirals Princess Carol Covert & her father, Frank Covert 7. 1981 Admirals Ball Queen Joan Granger escorted by Bob Duke 8. Sonia & Sam Wilson are ready for the Jewel Ball in 1981 "A Scottish Fortnight" 9. Mr. & Mrs. Frank Morris, Jr. 10. Liz Carpenter 11. Debbie Kitchen, Victor Costa, & Linda Washam

15

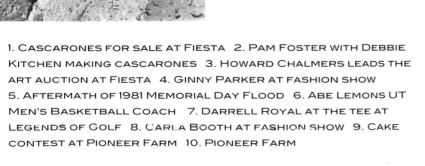

1. Cascarones for sale at Fiesta 2. Pam Foster with Debbie Kitchen making cascarones 3. Howard Chalmers leads the art auction at Fiesta 4. Ginny Parker at fashion show 5. Aftermath of 1981 Memorial Day Flood 6. Abe Lemons UT Men's Basketball Coach 7. Darrell Royal at the tee at Legends of Golf 8. Carla Booth at fashion show 9. Cake contest at Pioneer Farm 10. Pioneer Farm

2

CHAPTER TWO 1982–1987

During this period, the population of Travis County grew from 430,573 to 547,418. Bill Clements was governor until Mark White took office in 1983. Carol Rylander was mayor before handing over to Ron Mullen who was followed by Frank Cooksey. The economy was the big topic as it started to slump in 1986—growing worse in 1987 and staying bad until the early 90's.

1. Linda Burford 2. Teresa Cain 3. Jo Ann Merica
Junior Helping Hand fashion show 4. Maline MaCalla
5. Nancy Scott 6. Gray Hawn 7. Sharon Wilson bowing
at Junior Helping Hand 1982 8. The Texas Bow
9. Bob & Kay Lane 10. The Texas Bow 11. Children at the
Junior Helping Hand fashion show 1982

18

V ictoria Hentrich was becoming a party planner of renown in Austin in these years. Her planning was all-inclusive at the event with décor, entertainment and dining. She was the first to offer the "mashed potato martini" which allowed guests to decorate a martini glass of mashed potatoes with their choice of condiments. It has been a feature of innumerable parties ever since.

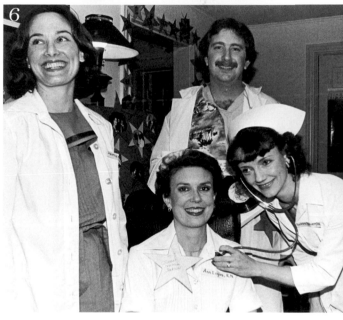

1. Bill Shoop, Jane Sibley, Sung Kwak, friend 2. Bud & Robin Shivers
3. Academy Awards party 4. Party planner Victoria Hentrich & client
5. Grethen Neff's Academy Awards party 6. Melissa Jackson being checked by Deborah Teten 7. Sarah & Ernest Butler 8. Ginny Parker at Symphony Style Show

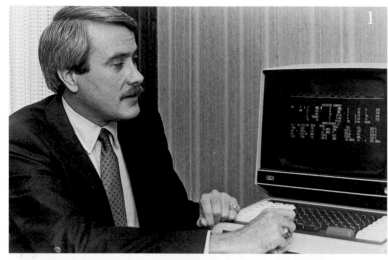

There was a fund-raiser for the Harry Ransom Center that brought two major celebrities into play. James Michener was joined by Walter Cronkite for the evening. Cronkite had just published a book "South by Southeast." My work that evening involved following the two men around and photographing them with any of the event's attendees. After doing this for about 90 minutes, they decided to take a break and sat down on a convenient couch. It was at that moment that Michener's wife, Mari, decided I needed to have my picture taken with Michener and Cronkite. She took my camera and shot the photo. Sad to say, it is underexposed and out of focus—but still highly prized by me.

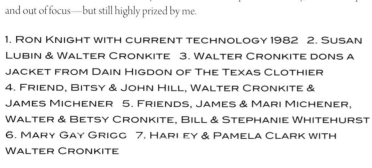

1. RON KNIGHT WITH CURRENT TECHNOLOGY 1982   2. SUSAN LUBIN & WALTER CRONKITE   3. WALTER CRONKITE DONS A JACKET FROM DAIN HIGDON OF THE TEXAS CLOTHIER
4. FRIEND, BITSY & JOHN HILL, WALTER CRONKITE & JAMES MICHENER   5. FRIENDS, JAMES & MARI MICHENER, WALTER & BETSY CRONKITE, BILL & STEPHANIE WHITEHURST
6. MARY GAY GRIGG   7. HARLEY & PAMELA CLARK WITH WALTER CRONKITE

1. MARY MARGARET FARABEE WITH JACK & NANCY COLLINS
2. RICHARD WAWRO & FANNIE LOU SPELCE 3. FANNIE LOU
SPELCE 1983 4. GAYLE HEIGHT 5. MARION MORE
6. ED BLUESTEIN & FRIEND 7. CARLA BOOTH WITH THE
"BIG BOW" LOOK OF 1983 8. FRED & DIANE AKERS WITH
FANNIE LOU SPELCE 9. LILLA & TOM EZELL 10. BETTY RAINEY

21

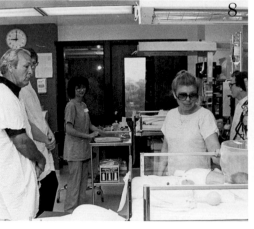

1. Cactus Pryor & Ken Koock 2. Fannie Lou Spelce & Eileen Sweatman 3. Amanda Beck & friend 4. Ben Barnes 5. Liz Carpenter, Chester Koock & Mary Faulk Koock 6. Arnold Palmer 7. Symphony Showhouses & Louis Nicholson (center) 8. Arnold Palmer visits the Children's Hospital 9. Damian Priour, friend, Horton Foote at Arthritis Benefit 1985

1. MARY & JACK BALAGIA 2. PATTI & DICK OBENHAUS
3. DAVID HUGHES WITH FRIENDS 4. DR. CHIP & KAREN
OSWALT 5. HOWARD CHALMERS AS AUCTIONEER
FOR KLRN 1984 6. PAULA & DAMIAN PRIOUR
7. JACK CAMPBELL & FRIEND 8. ROBERT & SHAY
SHOOP 9. BERYL & JAKE PICKLE WITH SALLY & BILL
WITTLIFF 10. ALICE & TONY SESSI AT ARTHRITIS
BENEFIT 11. BILL & REGAN GAMMON 12. JACK & NANCY
COLLINS 13. DAIN & LADONNA HIGDON 14. HOWARD &
MARY CHALMERS 15. BITSY HENDERSON & FRIEND

1. Carole & Ron Mullen at Junior Forum Spring Fling
2. Spring Fling 3. Cactus Pryor as a model 4-5. Spring
Fling 6 Mary Faulk Koock 7. Mary Pearl Williams
8. Linda Gale White

1. DAVID & MARTHA TILLER   2. LUCI JOHNSON   3. H.C. & JOAN CARTER   4. HELEN & MILTON SMITH

5. RAYE & WALTER CARRINGTON   6. T&Y & MIKE PATTON   7. SPENSER & NANCY SCOTT

8. ROBERTA JONES AT LBJ RANCH 1984   9. KAREN SPELLINGS WITH FRIENDS

10. DARRELL & EDITH ROYAL WITH ED BRUCE   11. LYNDA JOHNSON ROBB   12. HELEN HAYES

13. AMANDA BLAKE SPAETH & MARK SPAETH

1. VICKI ROAN, SUSAN LUBIN, DAIN HIGDON, FRIEND
2. MARGENE & PAT BECKAM   3. MEDICAL AUXILIARY 1985
4. TERESA CAIN & MARY KOCUREK   5. BETTY RAINEY
MODELING WITH FRIEND   6. DIANNE SCHOCH & GAYLE
CULLINGTON   7. A DOCTOR HAVING TO MODEL
8. CHILD MODEL   9. HETTY CLEMENTS   10. ALEXANDRA
NADAL   11. MARY LOU FITZPATRICK

1. DANNY & CHARLOTTE POUNDS 2. MOVIE STAR MOM
3. KATHRYN FLYNN WITH GRANDDAUGHTER, GRAY HAWN
4. PAULA & DAMIAN PRIOUR 5. GERALD MANN ON RIGHT
6. MOVIE STAR MOM 7. LOWELL LEBERMANN & LINDA GALE WHITE
8. TINA & WILL HOUSTON 9. SHERRY BUCHANAN
10. KAREN OSWALT 11. MARY & NEAL KOCUREK WITH CECILIA &
MERV COOK

1. DIANA KENDLE   2. BARBARA MINTON   3. RUTH ANN SPIVEY   4. MARY GAY GRIGG   5. JO ANNE CHRISTIAN   6. DOC SEVERINSEN WITH JANE & D.J. SIBLEY   7. ANN BUTLER & PHIL MAXWELL   8. DOUG & MARGARET DANFORTH, DOC SEVERINSEN, LINDA & JIM PRENTICE
9. ROBERT & NANCY BUFORD   10. BAILIE & BEVERLY GRIFFITH
11. TISH HALL

28

1. The Carol & Larry Niemann family   2. Betty Rainey,   3. Greg Kozmetsky family   4. Settlement Club Garage Sale—Kay Lane on right   5. Mike & Rebecca Levy & friend   6. Sharon Wilkes & Susan Klein   7. Oscar & Nancy Robinson with friends   8. Grand Opening of Simon David—Patti & Dick Obenhaus with friend   9. Jenny Link & friend

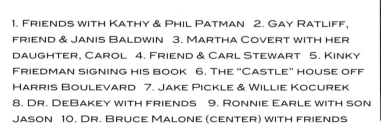

1. FRIENDS WITH KATHY & PHIL PATMAN   2. GAY RATLIFF, FRIEND & JANIS BALDWIN   3. MARTHA COVERT WITH HER DAUGHTER, CAROL   4. FRIEND & CARL STEWART   5. KINKY FRIEDMAN SIGNING HIS BOOK   6. THE "CASTLE" HOUSE OFF HARRIS BOULEVARD   7. JAKE PICKLE & WILLIE KOCUREK 8. DR. DEBAKEY WITH FRIENDS   9. RONNIE EARLE WITH SON JASON   10. DR. BRUCE MALONE (CENTER) WITH FRIENDS

1. ANN HANNA & FRANCES PEARCE 2. BOB & HETTY CLEMENTS 3. MIKE REYNOLDS & "ZEBRA CAR" 4. TERRY & DIANA KENDLE
5. LYRIC OPERA EVENT 1987 6. BILL CUNNINGHAM (RIGHT) 7. LORETTA VOSS, JILL TURLINGTON & SUE WEBER 8. ELSPETH & WALT ROSTOW & FRIEND 9. ALFRED & ELLEN KING
10. LIBBY MALONE WITH THE NEW JUNIOR LEAGUE COOKBOOK 11. SANDY PERKINS MODELING 12. JAN HUGHES, KATHY LINDAUER, DAVID HUGHES, MARY & CHARLES TEEPLE 13. DALE COKER MODELING

31

1. ALEC & AMANDA BECK WITH FRIENDS   2. JEFF VOGEL
(CENTER)   3. ARTHRITIS "BEACH PARTY"   4. FRIEND, MARILYN
FERGUSON, JOYCE ORR   5. PAMELA MAYO CLARK & BRAD
MEYER AT ARTHRITIS "BEACH PARTY"   6. JANE & MICHAEL
DRISCOLL & FRIEND   7. FRIEND WITH GAY & SHANNON RATLIFF
8. ROSE BETTY WILLIAMS, PAUL & PEGGY BROWN, PAUL BURNS
9. FRIEND WITH MALINE & DUDLEY MCCALLA   10. JARE & JIM
SMITH WITH FRIEND   11. BETTIE & BOB GIRLING

1. Eugene Slavin & Alexandra Nadal
2. Rogen Giles   3. Linda Ball & Forrest
Preece   4. Bob & Kay Lane   5. Ballet event
1987   6. Herk & Christine Wotkyns   7. Jare &
Jim Smith   8. Sonia & Sam Wilson   9. Nancy &
Oscar Robinson

33

1. ALAN & PATSY MINTER 2. AQUA FESTIVAL FLOAT
PARADE 3. SHERRY BUCHANAN, MISSY MOSCOE &
FRIEND 4. CINDY MCWILLIAMS MODELING 5. SUE &
FRANK MCBEE WITH KATHY & TIM LOWRY
6. STEPHANIE WILLIAMS MODELING 7. DALE & CHEY
COKER 8. SIDNEY & JOHN JONES 9. SUSAN & BOB
RICHARDSON 10. GAYLE & JIM CULLINGTON WITH
MARY BETH & STEVE MCMILLON

1. Jessie B Anderson & friend   2. Junior League modeling
3. Patti Riley Brown & Teresa Clark at Symphony Showhouse
4. Laura Pena & Mary Beth McMillon   5. Regan & Billy Gammon
6. Michelle Smith, fashion editor for American-Statesman
7. Mary Gay Grigg

1. Admirals Club Queen 1988 Lyndie Clements 2. Admirals Royalty Kate Cauthorn, Lyndie Clement & Allison Cook 3. Miss Austin Aqua Fest 1987 & Gary Melon 4. Coverts & friends at Admirals 5. Joy Scott, Hetty Clements & Bitsy Hill 6. Sissy Brown & friend 7. Beth Granger & friends 8. Chip & Karen Oswalt with Bob Clements

1. THE AMERICAN STATESMAN 10K RUN 1987   2. REBECCA LEVY
3. THE SWEARIGENS WITH THE THORNHILLS   4. FRIENDS WITH
KATHY RIDER & LIBBY MALONE   5. KAREN BOATRIGHT, TIM
HERMAN   6. SAFARI PARTY WITH ROSE MARIE HAGMAN (SECOND
FROM RIGHT)   7. WALLACE & LANETTE SMITH   8. FRIEND, MARY
HERMAN & JAN HUGHES   9. FRIEND, CINDY KOZMETSKY, &
MAUREEN BRITTON   10. WAYA EVENT WITH DEALEY HERNDON
(2D LEFT)

1. Nancy Norvell, friend, Lynn Brill & Mary Lyles
2. Carole & Ron Mullen   3. Maureen & Willie Kocurek
4. Janis & Robert Baldwin   5. The Charles Morrison family
6. Dick & Sarah Rathgeber   7. B J & Rooster Andrews
8. Kerry & Nancy Merritt   9. Sally Byram, Anne Hanna &
Robin Shivers

1. MARY MEYERS   2. CHARLES & MARY TEEPLE
3. PAT & MARGENE BECKHAM WITH SHARI & CAREY
BRENNAN   4. FRIEND, BARBARA & ROY MINTON &
SHARON HOOSER   5. PAGE KEETON, JIM BRAZY,
WILLIE & MAURINE KOCUREK   6. FRANCES NEAL,
ALISON HANKS, MARY GAY GRIGG   7. FRIEND,
DOROTHY VOSCOVO, NANCY WILSON & MARGARET
SCARBROUGH   8. JOE & SUE WEBER
9. KAY & JOHN BRAZIEL WITH MARGARET & DOUG
DANFORTH

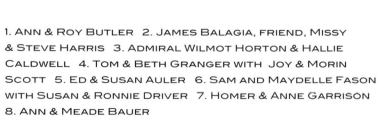

1. ANN & ROY BUTLER 2. JAMES BALAGIA, FRIEND, MISSY
& STEVE HARRIS 3. ADMIRAL WILMOT HORTON & HALLIE
CALDWELL 4. TOM & BETH GRANGER WITH JOY & MORIN
SCOTT 5. ED & SUSAN AULER 6. SAM AND MAYDELLE FASON
WITH SUSAN & RONNIE DRIVER 7. HOMER & ANNE GARRISON
8. ANN & MEADE BAUER

1. Admiral & Scott Carter 2. Linda Rowland
3. Friend, Joyce Orr, Mary Beth McMillon & Susan
Richardson 4. Bob Lowe & friends at Wine & Food
Festival 5. John & Keni Neff 6. Friend, Christine
Wotkyns & Sonja Holt 7. Earl Maxwell, Bob
Richardson & friend 8. Pam & Bruce Kneirim
9. James & Eve Fish with Wayne & Joan Holtzman
10. Marilyn Ferguson with Eugene Slavin &
Alexandra Nadal

41

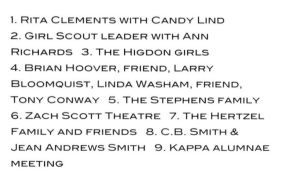

1. RITA CLEMENTS WITH CANDY LIND
2. GIRL SCOUT LEADER WITH ANN RICHARDS   3. THE HIGDON GIRLS
4. BRIAN HOOVER, FRIEND, LARRY BLOOMQUIST, LINDA WASHAM, FRIEND, TONY CONWAY   5. THE STEPHENS FAMILY
6. ZACH SCOTT THEATRE   7. THE HERTZEL FAMILY AND FRIENDS   8. C.B. SMITH & JEAN ANDREWS SMITH   9. KAPPA ALUMNAE MEETING

1. Alicean Kalteyer & Rose Betty Williams 2. Jerry Conn & Laurie Conn 3. Cindy & Gerald Stone 4. Williams Sonoma opening 5. Frances Pearce & her mother 6. Settlement Club Garage Sale with Hetty Owen & Martha Covert 7. Don Cox & friend 8. The Staff of the West Austin News in 1987 9. Damian Priour has art selected for the Huntington 10. 1886 Room volunteers including Greg Free (left)

1. KOCUREK FAMILY   2. MARY, SUZANNE & NEAL KOCUREK   3. SCOTT KIDD & DEE VARGAS   4. JEANNE DANIELS & MARY LEE CRUZEMAN   5. BACHELORS BALL 1987   6. GAY RATLIFF WITH ALAN & ROSE BETTY WILLIAMS   7. THE FIRST BACHELORS BALL AT THE OMNI 1987   8. YOUNG LADY WITH MARY MARGARET FARABEE

1. BETTY KING NOT LETTING A FOOT INJURY SLOW HER DOWN   2. BACHELORS BALL
3. MR. & MRS. ANDY FISH WITH LADY BIRD JOHNSON   4. CAROLYN CURTIS &
MALINE MCCALLA   5. DIAMOND QUEEN MARION FRANCIS MORE & KING BRIO XXII
ERNEST WALKER   6. JOHN & KENI NEFF   7. ELIZABETH WILLIAMS, FRIEND, JOYCE
ORR AT THE BACHELORS BALL   8. RICHARD & MARTHA COONS
9. WILLIE MAE & GEORGE STRANDTMAN

1. Ken & Debbie Kitchen   2. The Lettermen perform for
Children's Hospital   3. Lynn & Louis Brill   4. The Beckham
family   5. Karen & Chip Oswalt with Missy Gray
6. Paula Washburn   7. Symphony fashion show   8. Betty
Rainey   9. Janis Baldwin   10. Jo Anne Christian

1. Loretta Voss   2. Junior Forum Fling   3. Pam & George Willeford
4. Terry & Susan Parker   5. Jill & Lynn Turlington   6. Larry Laden
& Stephanie Williams   7. Bruce & Libby Malone   8. Frank & Melissa
Jackson   9. Jim & Gayle Cullington   10. Friend & Melissa Jackson

1. Thomas & Karen Vaughn with friend 2. Mary Faulk Koock 3. Children's Hospital committee meeting 4. Ann Wilson, Jeff Bridges, Susan & Ed Auler 5. Susan Lubin & Jeff Bridges 6. Jeff Bridges & Jill Turlington 7. Doug English with fans 8. Charlotte & Mike London with Janette Soeltje 9. Sug Danforth with Peggy & R.G. Mueller

48

1. ED & PAT HARRIS WITH FRIENDS   2. ROBIN & BUD SHIVERS
3. CAROL KEETON RYLANDER & HILL RYLANDER AT NATURAL
SCIENCE CENTER BENEFIT   4. MARY MARGARET FARABEE &
MALINE MCCALLA   5. LEE KELLY, BILL MOYERS, FRIEND, GRACE
JONES   6. FRIEND, JIM MATTOX, EDITH & DARRELL ROYAL
7. SUSAN RICHARDSON & SIDNEY JONES   8. NATURAL SCIENCE
CENTER BENEFIT   9. LADY BIRD JOHNSON WITH ALAN WRIGHT &
CUSTIS

1

2

3

5

6

4

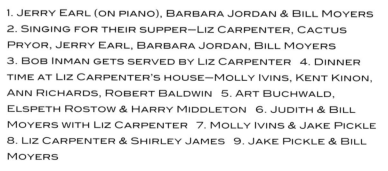

7

8

9

1. JERRY EARL (ON PIANO), BARBARA JORDAN & BILL MOYERS
2. SINGING FOR THEIR SUPPER—LIZ CARPENTER, CACTUS
PRYOR, JERRY EARL, BARBARA JORDAN, BILL MOYERS
3. BOB INMAN GETS SERVED BY LIZ CARPENTER 4. DINNER
TIME AT LIZ CARPENTER'S HOUSE—MOLLY IVINS, KENT KINON,
ANN RICHARDS, ROBERT BALDWIN 5. ART BUCHWALD,
ELSPETH ROSTOW & HARRY MIDDLETON 6. JUDITH & BILL
MOYERS WITH LIZ CARPENTER 7. MOLLY IVINS & JAKE PICKLE
8. LIZ CARPENTER & SHIRLEY JAMES 9. JAKE PICKLE & BILL
MOYERS

1. LIZ'S MENU 2. PATRICIA PATTERSON & LOWELL LEBERMANN 3. LADY BIRD JOHNSON WITH PATRICIA PATTERSON & LOWELL LEBERMANN 4. SHIRLEY JAMES & LIZ CARPENTER WITH POLITICAL AGENDA 5. JOHN HENRY FAULK ARRIVES 6. JAMES ARMSTRONG ARRIVES 7. CACTUS PRYOR & ANN RICHARDS 8. BILL HOBBY WITH PATRICIA PATTERSON & LOWELL LEBERMANN

1. CHARLES & SYLVIA BETTS WITH FOREST ROAN & FRIEND
2. BARBARA VACKAR, JOYCE SHELTON & JOYCE BROYLES
3. EDEN & HAL BOX   4. GRACE JONES & LORETTA YOUNG
5. BETTY KIRK, MARK WHITE & HART PETERSON
6. FRIEND, ALICEAN KALTEYER, RUTH KOHLHAAS & CHUCK
KALTEYER   7. RON & CHRIS ATTAL   8. KATHERYN & JOHN
BERNARDONI   9. BEN BARNES & JOHN HILL
10. MARGARET PERRY WITH BILL & SUZON KEMP
11. JUDY MOORE, KATHY PLATT & MELBA MCINTOSH

52

1. LORETTA YOUNG 2. BISHOP WITH LORETTA YOUNG & GRACE JONES 3. JANE SIBLEY, NANCY SCOTT & HETTY CLEMENTS 4. JANE SIBLEY MODELING 5. MARION MORE, HELEN BOSTICK, JANE SIBLEY & PEGGY BROWN 6. SYMPHONY FASHION LEADERS IN 1987 7. HARRY MIDDLETON & GRACE JONES

53

1. KEN & DEBBIE KITCHEN, TONY CONWAY, MARTHA & RICHARD COONS 2. SCOTTY & JULIE SAYERS WITH MARY ANN & BRYAN SAYERS 3. SHELLY PAGE, AMANDA BECK & GAY GADDIS 4. VICKIE & MARK EIDMAN 5. JILL TURLINGTON, CINDY STONE & DIANE DOPSON

1. ALICE & TONY SESSI 2. FRIEND, AMY WILSON, PAMELA MAYO CLARK 3. LANA & MR. WILSON 4. MARTHA & RICHARD COONS 5. FRED & SHERRY DAVIS 6. SYMPHONY SHOWHOUSE COMMITTEE 7. PAULA & DAMIAN PRIOUR

1. SUZY BALAGIA & CHRISTINA WEEKS
2. VICTORIA HENTRICH & FRIEND   3. GREG
KOZMETSKY AT ST. EDWARD'S UNIVERSITY 1985
4. IDEE KWAK & NANCY MCCOY   5. ERIN & ROY
METRANEK   6. KAY LANE & NANCY MCCOY
7. PAT HAYES AT ST. EDWARD'S UNIVERSITY
1985

56

3

CHAPTER THREE 1988–1993

During this period, the population of Travis County grew from 547,418 to over 600,000. Bill Clements was again governor before Ann Richards began her term. Lee Cooke was mayor before handing over to Bruce Todd. The local economy was in terrible shape at the beginning of this period, but recovered in the early 90's with the "tech bubble."

1. DAVID & JOYCE ORR WITH MARILYN & MALCOLM FERGUSON—BALLET GALA 1988 2. DON WILDER WITH RENEE & EDWARD BUTLER 1988 3. CHARLES & MARY TEEPLE WITH LEE COOKE 4. PAUL BROWN SERVING GRACE & BRIAN SOKOLIK 5. PEGGY BROWN & SUSAN AULER AT LYRIC OPERA WINE TASTING 1988 6. KENT LANCE & SUSAN DELL AT PIKE POWERS ROAST 7. CAROLYN BENGTSON WITH MARK WHITE 1988 8. HYDE PARK YOUNGSTERS ENJOY DISCOVERY HALL

58

1. Pike Powers enjoys his roasting 1988 2. Heart Association celebrity waiters 3. Jeff & Missy Gray at Ronald McDonald House benefit 4. Sarah Weddington & Mary Pearl Williams 5. Ben Vereen performs 6. Friend with Marilyn Roberts & Eddie Smith at showhouse 7. Shirley Hanslik, Jean Marie Giegerich-Schnurr, Richard & Martha Coons 1988 8. Linda Gray at Junior Helping Hand fashion show 9. Dee Vargas, Sidney Jones & friend

1. HERK & CHRISTINE WOTKYNS 2. JOYCE & JIM PRENTICE
3. BETTY & BILL KING WITH JO ANNE & GEORGE
CHRISTIAN FEBRUARY 1988 4. BETH ATHERTON 5. DICK
RATHGEBER 6. HAZEL RANSOM & ISABELLA CUNNINGHAM
1988 7. ANN MOODY & MARY TOWNSEND 8. WROE
JACKSON AT JUNIOR HELPING HAND FASHION SHOW 1988
9. COUPLE WITH MR. & MRS. DANIELS 10. MACEY &
HARRY REASONER

1. Mr. & Mrs. Smith, Nancy Norvell & Ann Norman 2. Frank Cooksey & Candice Bergan 3. George Christian 4. Isamu Taniguchi (left) of Zilker Garden fame & friend 5. Kathy Cronkite at celebrity waiter benefit 1988 6. Longhorns at the Capitol 7. Brooke & Sally Byram with Lynn Brill 8. Friend, Father Richard McCabe & Leo Herzog 9. Friend, Terry Sasser, Beryl & Jake Pickle

1. Robin & Bud Shivers   2. Tom Penders with Nellie & John Connally   3. Fans with Larry L King & Sally Wittliff
4. Stephanie & Bill Whitehurst   5. Gina & Walter Ducloux
6. Gay & Lee Gaddis   7. Ian Turpin, Luci Johnson, Surrenden & Russell Roby   8. Bob & Penny Powell   9. Bill Wittliff

62

1. FRIEND & JERRY JEFF WALKER 2. AL &
MARY ANN GOLDEN WITH SHAY & ROBERT
SHOOP 3. SPENSER & NANCY SCOTT
4. GLENN CAMPBELL, DEBBIE & KEN
KITCHEN, FRIEND AT CATTLE BARONS
BALL 1988 5. ROBIN & BUD SHIVERS 6.
LINDA & ROBERT ROWLAND 7. NANCY &
KERRY MERRIT 8. ALEC & AMANDA BECK
9. LAURENS & JULIA FISH

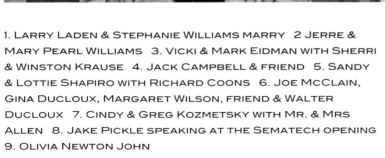

1. LARRY LADEN & STEPHANIE WILLIAMS MARRY 2 JERRE &
MARY PEARL WILLIAMS 3. VICKI & MARK EIDMAN WITH SHERRI
& WINSTON KRAUSE 4. JACK CAMPBELL & FRIEND 5. SANDY
& LOTTIE SHAPIRO WITH RICHARD COONS 6. JOE MCCLAIN,
GINA DUCLOUX, MARGARET WILSON, FRIEND & WALTER
DUCLOUX 7. CINDY & GREG KOZMETSKY WITH MR. & MRS
ALLEN 8. JAKE PICKLE SPEAKING AT THE SEMATECH OPENING
9. OLIVIA NEWTON JOHN

1. GATHERING FOR THE SEMATECH OPENING   2. AMY JENNESS
DAVIS   3. TOMMY & THEO COWAN WITH DENNIS & LOU COWAN
4. CURTIS PAGE, AMANDA BECK & FRIEND FOR ARTHRITIS
FOUNDATION   5. TERRELL SMITH & JESSICA   6. KAY &
CHARLES FINLEY   7. STACIE & LOUIS NICHOLSON   8. KATHY
ALLEN, PAT BULLOCK, FRIEND, SUSAN RICHARDSON

1. CHILDREN'S HOSPITAL COMMITTEE 1989
2. FRIEND, GUEST STAR, LAVADA JACKSON &
NEAL SPELCE   3. ROY METRANEK WITH STACIE
& LOUIS NICHOLSON   4. ALEC MCMILLON
(RIGHT) AS CHILD MODEL   5. HEADLINERS CLUB
6. VICKIE & GLENN WEST   7. BARBARA
MILLER WITH JANET & JEDAN HOOTEN   8. TWO
FELLOWS WITH GIB LEWIS

1. JOHN & GENE ANN SANDBACH 2. JAMES & SARA FLIELLER AT CENTER FOR BATTERED WOMEN EVENT 1989 3. LEE COOKE, BARBARA VACKER COOKE, KATHLEEN & FRANK NIENDORFF 4. CYNDY PERKINS, ERIN TASSOULAS & KAREN OSWALT 5. FRIEND, PAUL BEUTEL, & FRIENDS 6. JEFF GRAY, LIZ CARPENTER, AUDREY BATEMAN & JOHN SCURLOCK 7. WENDY LINEHAN, DEBRA SEWELL, PAT BULLOCK, DEBBIE DAVIS, MANETTE SCANIO AND EVENT CHAIR SHERRI KRAUSE FOR NATURAL SCIENCE CENTER 8. ANN RICHARDS, GENE FONDREN & BETTY KING 9. BAILIE & BEVERLY GRIFFITH 10. HOWARD & MARY CHALMERS

1. Dick & Sarah Rathgeber with Louis & Lynn Brill
2. A collection of fabric prints in 1989   3. Friends with
Linda & Jim Prentice   4. Oscar, Ann & Nancy Robinson
5. Sofia & Jack Balagia & friends & family   6. Susan &
Terry Parker with Susan Driver   7. Bill Hobby with
Vickie & Ron Kessler   8. Jan & Bob Bullock   9. Steve
McKee, Marcia Ball & MariBen Ramsey

1. MARK RUSSELL APPEARING FOR KLRU
2. EARL & ANITA MAXWELL GAMBLING FOR CHARITY   3. JULIE & BEN CRENSHAW WITH FRIEND   4. SHERRY BUCHANAN & MISSY MOSCOE   5. JOE MCCLAIN, FRIEND & ALEC TREBEC FOR LYRIC OPERA IN MAY 1989   6. TERESA & JOE LONG   7. FIESTA POSTER 1989 WITH ROSE BETTY WILLIAMS & ARTIST A. D. GREER   8. TONI & PAUL BURNS
9. DAVE & AMY DAVIS WITH KAY & BOB LANE
10. NANCY & SPENSER SCOTT

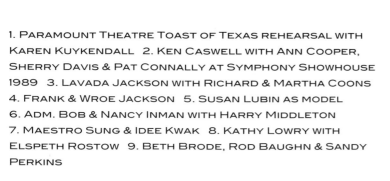

1. PARAMOUNT THEATRE TOAST OF TEXAS REHEARSAL WITH KAREN KUYKENDALL 2. KEN CASWELL WITH ANN COOPER, SHERRY DAVIS & PAT CONNALLY AT SYMPHONY SHOWHOUSE 1989 3. LAVADA JACKSON WITH RICHARD & MARTHA COONS 4. FRANK & WROE JACKSON 5. SUSAN LUBIN AS MODEL 6. ADM. BOB & NANCY INMAN WITH HARRY MIDDLETON 7. MAESTRO SUNG & IDEE KWAK 8. KATHY LOWRY WITH ELSPETH ROSTOW 9. BETH BRODE, ROD BAUGHN & SANDY PERKINS

1. Ribbon cutting at Ronald McDonald House with Sally Shipman in May 1989   2. King Brio XXIV Wayne & Joan Holtzman   3. Roy & Barbara Minton with Bettie & Bob Girling
4. Henri Coleman at Symphony Fashion Show September 1989   5. Friend with Penny Reeves
6. Alan & Patsy Minter   7. Corey & Patty Hoffpauir with Ben & Julie Crenshaw   8. Daryl Howard & Owen
9. Friend with Beverly Daugherty   10. Sherry Davis, Linda Washam & Susan Ducloux

1. Suzanne Kocurek & Neal Kocurek 2. Ian Turpin, Lady Bird Johnson & Luci Johnson 3. The Niemann girls—Nancy, Connie & Sherry at Bachelors Ball November 1989 4. Alicean Kalteyer & her work 5. Amanda & Alec Beck 6. Curtis Page Family 7. Margaret Murchison & stepdad Louis Brill 8. Pam & Pike Powers 9. Bachelors Ball 1989

72

1. Friend with Doyle & Claireen Fellers   2. Joy Hawn, Greer Evans & Gray Hawn   3. D. J. & Jane Sibley   4. Dain & LaDonna Higdon   5. Robert & Lutie Butler   6. Kay Stowell & friend   7. Friend & Frank Morris   8. Mr. & Mrs. Andy Fish at A Christmas Affair 1989   9. Jeanette & Ferris Nassour   10. Jane Parker, friend, friend & Pat Connally at Settlement Club Garage Sale 1989

1. DONNA LOPIANO & BETTY HIMMELBLAU
AT BLACK TIE TENNIS 1989   2. JO ANNE
CHRISTIAN, PATTI RILEY BROWN & FRIEND
3. MARGARET & DOUG DANFORTH
4. LAMBROS LAMBROU, ARTISTIC DIRECTOR
AT BALLET AUSTIN 1989   5. LOWELL
LEBERMANN, HAGEN MCMAHON & BUD
SHIVERS   6. COMMITTEE GATHERING 1989   7.
SHOAL CREEK HOSPITAL 20TH BIRTHDAY
8. ST. MICHAELS SCHOOL BENEFIT 1989   9.
MERV & CECILIA COOK
10. VICKI EIDMAN, SALLIE STARKER, STEVE
THOMPSON & JOYCE PRENTICE

1. GERALD McCoy, KATHLEEN McCoy &
NANCY McCoy AT JUNIOR HELPING HAND
ANNOUNCEMENT 1990 2. JILL TURLINGTON,
STACY TURLINGTON & LYNN TURLINGTON
3. AWARDS PRESENTED TO BILL HUFFMAN & MARY
McDANIEL 4. NOEL GATHERING 1990 5. NANCY
DUNCAN, CHARLOTTE GRES, GWEN SCOTT &
SHIRLEY PRUDHOMME 6. KATHLEEN & FRANK
NIENDORFF & SONS AT CHRISTMAS 1989 7. MARY
YANCY, MARILYN MOORE & ERIN TASSOULAS
8. BARBARA JASPER, MATHA BENGTSON & LINDA
DAVIS

1. KATHLEEN NIENDORFF & STEPHANIE WHITEHURST 2. PAUL HILGERS & BILL HILGERS 3. CLAUDE & SUSAN DUCLOUX & FRIENDS 4. MARY LYLES, MARGARET MURCHISON & LYNN BRILL 5. ELLEN RICHARDS, SALLY WITTLIFF, FRIEND & ANN RICHARDS 6. KENI & JOHN NEFF WITH FRIEND AT 50'S PARTY 7. PIKE & PAM POWERS 8. HELEN & ED BAXTER 9. RAY & MARY MARGARET FARABEE 10. REBECCA & BRIAN HARDEMAN

1. Mary Beth & Steve McMillon 2. Laurie Hall with Bob & Virginia Duke 3. Gerald & Cindy Stone 4. Edith & Darrell Royal 5. Ed & Susan Auler 1990 6. Layton & Ann Wilson 7. Eva Gayle & George Gibbs 8. John Byram leads a tour for the Bachelors Club in January 1990 9. Mr. & Mrs. Hugh Lewis 10. Sam Donaldson & Jack Warren 11. Gene Attal with Mr. & Mrs. Batterton

1. PEGGY & CACTUS PRYOR   2. MARGIE, NELL, EVELYN & SHIRLEY   3. EMMETT & JOYCE SHELTON AT COSTUME PARTY   4. BETTY KING & WILLIE MAE STRANDTMAN   5. JACK & NANCY COLLINS WITH PAT & CAROL ROBERTSON   6. JEWEL BALL COMMITTEE MEETING   7. CAROLE KEETON MAKING NOTES   8. JEWEL BALL DECORATIONS WORK 1990

1. Edward Fowler surrounded by friends   2. Lutie & Robert Butler at Admirals Ball 1990   3. Doug & Dorothy Nichols   4. Frank & Charmaine Denius   5. Jack & Doris Dealey   6. A seated Mr. Gammage with friends   7. Pris Flawn, Barbara Gaines & Peter Flawn   8. Bradley Bengtson & his grandmother, Minnie Seay   9. Robin & Bud Shivers, Bill & Isabella Cunningham, friend, Barbara Gaines

1. John & Nellie Connally with Peter Flawn   2. George & Eva Gayle Gibbs, Pamela Gibbs, Dale Mila   3. Young couple with Harriet & Ted Nagel   4. Frank Denius & the ribbon cutting for the UT Alumni Center September 1990   5. Charles & Mary Lou Morrison   6. Jodie & Dave Smith   7. A group of young Austinites

1. Stephanie Williams, Sue Weber, Patti Obenhaus, Toni Burns 2. Mardi Gras party 3. Patti Obenhaus, Toni Burns, Mary Ann Brindley, friend, Jo Anne Christian 4. Karen Oswalt as a model 5. Bitsy Henderson as a model 6. Jo Anne Christian, Betty King, Janet Stoeltje, Sonia Wilson 7. Gary & Joni Raba

1. FRED & SHERRY DAVIS WITH RICK & GINNY PARKER
2. AMY ROAN & VICKI ROAN   3. KING BRIO XXV SAM &
SONIA WILSON   4. STEVE WILSON & FRIEND   5. AMELIA
BULLOCK & BILL CRUMPACK   6. HALINA PRADZINSKY
WITH HER HUSBAND ANDRE   7. LANA WILSON WITH
HOMER & ANNE GARRISON   8. JANET & JOE HOOTEN
9. BOBBIE GIRLING WITH BETTIE GIRLING

1. Marcia & David Caldwell for Pioneer Farm Fall Festival 1990 2. Anita Maxwell & Penny Powell 3. Vickie & Kerry Pollard 4. Beryl & Jake Pickle at a hoedown 5. Barbara & Alston Boyd, Loretta Marsh, Ellen Aiello 6. George Meriwether, Angie & Charles Umlauf & Sara Meriwether 7. V.C. Smart, James Michener, Dorothy Winters 8. Dick & Gail Williams with Lolla & Billy Page 9. Mr. & Mrs. Douglas with Shirley & Karl Umlauf

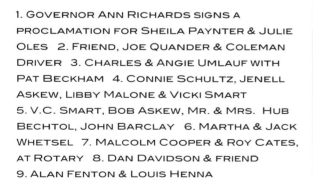

1. Governor Ann Richards signs a proclamation for Sheila Paynter & Julie Oles   2. Friend, Joe Quander & Coleman Driver   3. Charles & Angie Umlauf with Pat Beckham   4. Connie Schultz, Jenell Askew, Libby Malone & Vicki Smart
5. V.C. Smart, Bob Askew, Mr. & Mrs. Hub Bechtol, John Barclay   6. Martha & Jack Whetsel   7. Malcolm Cooper & Roy Cates, at Rotary   8. Dan Davidson & friend
9. Alan Fenton & Louis Henna

1

2

3

4

5

6

7

8

A momentous occasion in this period was the creation of the Umlauf Sculpture Garden and Museum. Nestled across the street from Zilker Park, the garden is an oasis filled with sculptures from the nationally renowned Charles Umlauf. An annual Garden Party is a significant fund raiser for the Garden.

1. EMILY STUBBS & HER FATHER PAUL STUBBS 1991 2. SYMPHONY BELLES & BEAUX 1992 3. JEWEL DIAMOND LYNN ELLEN SCARBROUGH ARRIVES IN STYLE 1992 4. MANAGING THE JEWEL CAPE & CROWN OF DIAMOND LYNN ELLEN SCARBROUGH AS SUPERVISED BY ALICE SCARBROUGH
5. BRENDA SCHOLIN, JOHN CONNALLY, NEAL SPELCE & NELLIE CONNALLY 6. KING BRIO XXVII SANDY & LOTTIE SHAPIRO
7. BOWLING FOR DOLLARS TO BENEFIT TRAVIS COUNTY MEDICAL AUXILARY 1989
8.MS. SANTINE, BETTY NUGENT & SUSAN PARKER WITH FLOWER FUNDRAISER

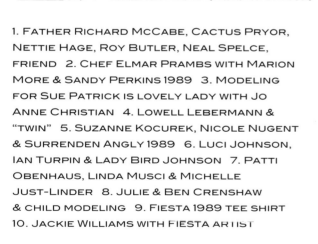

1. Father Richard McCabe, Cactus Pryor, Nettie Hage, Roy Butler, Neal Spelce, friend 2. Chef Elmar Prambs with Marion More & Sandy Perkins 1989 3. Modeling for Sue Patrick is lovely lady with Jo Anne Christian 4. Lowell Lebermann & "twin" 5. Suzanne Kocurek, Nicole Nugent & Surrenden Angly 1989 6. Luci Johnson, Ian Turpin & Lady Bird Johnson 7. Patti Obenhaus, Linda Musci & Michelle Just-Linder 8. Julie & Ben Crenshaw & child modeling 9. Fiesta 1989 tee shirt 10. Jackie Williams with Fiesta artist

BENEFITING
CHILDREN'S
HOSPITAL

FEATURING

THE SPINNERS

1. MAX NOFZIGER & FRIENDS   2. MICHAEL & SUSAN DELL 1989
3. BRUCE & LIBBY MALONE   4. RON OLIVEIRA, LORRAINE ADAMS &
FRIEND 5. A COUPLE OF FRIENDS WITH JANIE & TRUMAN BREED
6. JEANNE HOISINGTON, RON FRANKLIN, VAN HOISINGTON,
BONNIE FRANKLIN   7. NEAL & MARY KOCUREK   8. PIERRE &
ANGELA FILARDI   9. LILLA & TOM EZELL

1. WALTER & GINA DUCLOUX   2. PATTY HUFFINES,
PAM WILLEFORD, SUZY FIELDS, JUDY AVERY & GAIL
WILLIAMS STUFFING INVITATIONS FOR BANDANA
BALL BENEFITING THE RONALD MCDONALD HOUSE
3. MARY ELLEN & BETHEA BRINDLEY. 4. FRANK &
JANET ARNOLD 5. KAREN HERTEL, KAY BAILEY
HUTCHINSON, JULIE OLES & SONJA HOLT 6. TED &
HARRIET NAGEL WITH LOWELL LEBERMANN
7. STEVIE RAY VAUGHAN & BROTHER, JIMMY
VAUGHAN PLAY A PARTY 8. THE GREGORY
BROTHERS OF RED TOMATO FAME

1. New van for the Assistance League   2. Lolla Page, Marty Jastrow & Susie Jastrow   3. Bachelors Club debutantes 1990   4. Beth Voorhees & Sonja Holt   5. Kathleen Niendorff, friends, James Flieller & Karen Oswalt   6. Elizabeth Hibbetts & Nell Tanner at hat contest   7. Bob & Judy Mettlan & friend   8. Hat contest contestants 1991   9. Anne Garrison, Kay McHorse, & friend, Sally Meschan

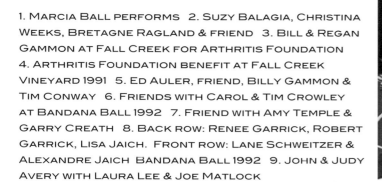

1. Marcia Ball performs 2. Suzy Balagia, Christina Weeks, Bretagne Ragland & friend 3. Bill & Regan Gammon at Fall Creek for Arthritis Foundation 4. Arthritis Foundation benefit at Fall Creek Vineyard 1991 5. Ed Auler, friend, Billy Gammon & Tim Conway 6. Friends with Carol & Tim Crowley at Bandana Ball 1992 7. Friend with Amy Temple & Garry Creath 8. Back row: Renee Garrick, Robert Garrick, Lisa Jaich. Front row: Lane Schweitzer & Alexandre Jaich Bandana Ball 1992 9. John & Judy Avery with Laura Lee & Joe Matlock

1. Pete & Tomi Winstead with Jim & Jare Smith
2. Kathy Girling, friend, Peggy Brown, Suzon Kemp, Beverly Daugherty, Willie Mae Strandtman, Marilyn Ferguson 3. Roy & Barbara Minton   4. B J & Rooster Andrews
5. Joe McClain with friends & staff at the new Lyric Opera building 6. Jan Lehman leads the laughs 7. George Christian, Jake Pickle, Darrell Royal, Frank Denius & friend
8. Cactus Pryor, Roy Butler & Lowell Lebermann 9. Friends of Harvey Penick & honoree Jake Pickle 10. Charles & Alicean Kalteyer

1. ADMIRALS CLUB MEMBERS INCLUDING JAMES HUFFINES (RIGHT) 2. ROBERT & ANN HUTHNANCE, ROBERT & BECKY HEISER, JUDY & RICKY ALEXANDER 3. LADY BIRD JOHNSON, DEBUTANTE & LUCI JOHNSON 4. DALE & CHEY COKER WITH FRIEND 5. BEAUTIFUL DEBUTANTE WITH WILL & TINA HOUSTON 6. FRANK & NINA SEELY 7. VICKY & AMY ROAN 8. GENE FONDREN & AMY WILSON 9. CAMILLE ABBOTT & FRIENDS

A particular moment of terror was taking the photo of Barbara Jordan with Ray Charles. I have a tremendous regard for Barbara Jordan so I certainly didn't want to disappoint her. I was at the Paramount for their annual gala when someone came up to me and said I was needed backstage to take the photo. The backstage wings of the Paramount are very narrow and dark as a dungeon. I could sense Barbara Jordan was as excited as a teenage schoolgirl at this photo op—but I couldn't see to focus! I guessed at the focus, had time to take two frames before being ushered away. This was in the film days, so I had to wait until I got to the darkroom before finding out that I had the shot.

1. GATHERED FOR A CAUSE 2. HARRIET MURPHY, BRENDA KENNEDY & FRIEND 3. BARBARA JORDAN & RAY CHARLES AT THE PARAMOUNT 4. JOINING FORCES 5. RAY CHARLES SURROUNDED BY FANS 6. VIRGINIA & SONNY WALLACE 7. THOSE DECORATIONS DON'T MAKE THEMSELVES

1. RON & SHEILA PAYNTER (CENTER) WITH FRIENDS   2. MINA BREES, EDDIE SAFADY, CAROL THOMPSON, HARLEY CLARK   3. RAY & MARY MARGARET FARABEE   4. THE AULERS RECEIVE AN AWARD FROM PREVENT BLINDNESS   5. PARAMOUNT GALA COMMITTEE WITH RAY CHARLES
6. RICK PERRY, FRIEND, VICKIE & RON KESSLER

1. PARAMOUNT GALA COMMITTEE WITH BEN VEREEN
2. BONNIE & CLYDE SMITH & FRIENDS   3. TROY KIMMEL, TAM ROGERS & FRIEND   4. TOODY BYRD, NANCY INMAN & FRIEND   5. CHARLIE & ROBERTA CRENSHAW WITH EMILY LITTLE   6. PAMELA & MIKE WARD AT HERITAGE SOCIETY
7. KAREN OSWALT & DAVID HUGHES

1. CLAUDE & SUSAN DUCLOUX 2. A GATHERING OF
BALLET AUSTIN FANS WITH ANN DOWNING & AUDREY
BATEMAN (RIGHT) 3. ELIZABETH GOODWIN OF ELLE
AMIE 4. GINA DUCLOUX WITH JOE & TERESA LONG
5. JO ANNE CHRISTIAN, ELLEN KING, DOYLE &
CLAIREEN FELLERS 6. FRIEND AND MARGARET
PARKER 7. SAM WILSON, TOM KITE & HARVEY PENICK

4 CHAPTER FOUR 1994–1999

During this time, the population of Travis County grew from just over 700,000 to just over 800,000. Ann Richards was governor before giving way to George Bush. Bruce Todd was mayor before yielding to Kirk Watson. The "tech bubble" burst, ending a flow of 7-digit non-profit donations.

1. Ian Turpin, Gerald Mann, friend, Terry Anderson,
Luci Johnson, friend at An Evening With Terry Anderson
2. Fred & Beth Voorhees with Lynn & Bill Fowler
3. Tish & Frank Hall   4. The New Texas Festival begins
which eventually yielded Conspirare of international
acclaim   5. Jan Hughes, Sarah Bird, David Lindsey,
Larry Wright & David Hughes at a Toast of the Town
party benefiting the St. David's Foundation 1994   6. Friend
with Jennene Mashburn   7. Frank Jackson & Alec Beck
8. The ribbon cutting for Tramex Travel with
Margo Portillo, Lidia Agraz, John Myers & Juan Portillo

1. GATHERED FOR BALLET AUSTIN: FRIEND, FRIEND, GAYLE HERRING, BONNIE DODGE, FRIEND 2. STEPHEN & DEBORAH JURCO (NOW YURCO) WITH KENI & JOHN NEFF 3. KENDYL RICHARDS & DOUG ENGLISH AT BRACKENRIDGE FOUNDATION CELEBRITY WAITER BENEFIT 4. MERCE WHITTINGTON, JO ANNE CHRISTIAN, LILLA ANN PARKER & ELLEN KING 5. JERRY TURNER, ALFRED KING, SCOTT THOMAS, JR. & DAN BULLOCK 6. JOHN & SAMIA JOSEPH IN 1994 AT A BRACKENRIDGE FOUNDATION BENEFIT 7. FRANCES PEARCE WITH HER PARENTS, CLEMMIE & JOHN BARCLAY 8. CHUCK MEYER & JACK BROWN

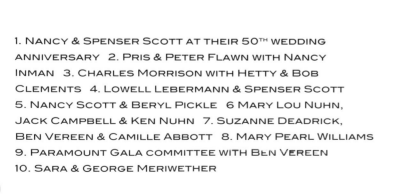

1. NANCY & SPENSER SCOTT AT THEIR 50TH WEDDING ANNIVERSARY   2. PRIS & PETER FLAWN WITH NANCY INMAN   3. CHARLES MORRISON WITH HETTY & BOB CLEMENTS   4. LOWELL LEBERMANN & SPENSER SCOTT 5. NANCY SCOTT & BERYL PICKLE   6 MARY LOU NUHN, JACK CAMPBELL & KEN NUHN   7. SUZANNE DEADRICK, BEN VEREEN & CAMILLE ABBOTT   8. MARY PEARL WILLIAMS 9. PARAMOUNT GALA COMMITTEE WITH BEN VEREEN 10. SARA & GEORGE MERIWETHER

1. WES HARLEY & WALLY SCOTT   2. SHAY & ROBERT SHOOP WITH
DAUGHTER, AMANDA SHOOP   3. WALTER & GINA DUCLOUX, JO ANNE
CHRISTIAN, HARRY ULLMANN & PETER SCHRAM   4. CRAIG HELLA
JOHNSON & DEACON CRAIN   5. TEXAS TOAST BENEFITING THE
PARAMOUNT THEATRE   6. DON COOK & PEGGY PICKLE AT LYRIC OPERA
EVENT   7. TEXAS TOAST BENEFITING THE PARAMOUNT THEATRE
8. DEBBI HEAD & KAREN SONLEITNER AT THE RHINESTONE CAMPOUT
1995   9. DICK JOHNSON, JANET STOELTJE, PETER & PRIS FLAWN

1-6 Texas Toast benefiting the Paramount Theatre 7. Texas Toast benefiting the Paramount Theatre· Kay Broline & Paul Beutel

1. STUFFING INVITATIONS FOR THE RONALD MCDONALD HOUSE BANDANA BALL: MARION MORE, JUDY AVERY, CAROL SCHWEITZER & CAROL ROBERTSON 2. JUDY & JOHN AVERY AT BANDANA BALL 3. STEPHANIE WILLIAMS & DAUGHTER AT AUSTIN WOMEN'S CENTER EASTER TEA 4. AUSTIN CHILDREN'S SHELTER WITH BURRELL JOHNSON (CENTER) 5. FANS OF THE RONALD MCDONALD HOUSE 6. JERAN & JANET HOOTEN WITH MISSY & N D MOSCOE 7. BRUCE KNIERIM, PAULA COOPWOOD, AMADO PENA, &FRIENDS 8. BILL & ISABELLA CUNNINGHAM 9. LUCY NAZRO & DEALEY HERNDON 10. AUGIE GARRIDO& CACTUS PRYOR 11. PHIL KOHLHAAS & ROBERTA CRENSHAW

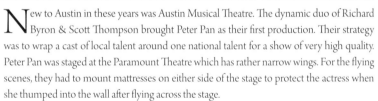

New to Austin in these years was Austin Musical Theatre. The dynamic duo of Richard Byron & Scott Thompson brought Peter Pan as their first production. Their strategy was to wrap a cast of local talent around one national talent for a show of very high quality. Peter Pan was staged at the Paramount Theatre which has rather narrow wings. For the flying scenes, they had to mount mattresses on either side of the stage to protect the actress when she thumped into the wall after flying across the stage.

1. John Adams, Bob Girling & Ron Mullen as King Brio
2. Wally Pryor & Gregory Hines 3. Missy Moscoe
with Gina & Walter Ducloux 4. Austin Musical
Theatre's Peter Pan with Linda Raman 5. Paramount
Theatre in November 1996 6. Friends with Betty
Buckley & Nina Seely 7. The start of Austin Musical
Theatre with Paul Beutel, Richard Byron, Linda Raman
& Scott Thompson in October 1996 8. Paul Beutel
& Betty Buckley 9. Ready for the Paramount Gala:
friend, friend, Scarlett Lewis, Nina Seely & friend

1. Committee gathering with: Karen Johnson, Debbie Kitchen, Martha Coons, Missy Moscoe, Susan Richardson, friend, Jeanne Hoisington & friend
2. B Ann Ballanfonte (right) & friend   3. Lady Bird Johnson at Headliners Club 1996   4. Ed & Helen Baxter, Dain & LaDonna Higdon, & Mary Ellen Borgelt
5. Admiring the art at Austin Country club
6. Jack Blanton & Lady Bird Johnson
7. Lady Bird Johnson & Elspeth Rostow   8. For St. David's: David Hughes, Alfred King, Nona Nil and, Hector Morales & Jack Campbell   9. Linda Prentice with Helen & Ed Baxter

CHILDREN'S HOSPITAL GALA 1. SUSAN & MICHAEL DELL 1997 2. NANCY GARRISON & MARGARET WILSON 3. JOE & LAURA LEE MATLOCK 4. DENISE GAMINO, GEORGE BUSH AND LAURA GAMINO   5. GARY & CINDY VALDEZ WITH ELLEN RICHARDS & EDDIE SAFADY 6. JOE & TERESA LONG, NINA SEELY, SCARLETT LEWIS, FRIEND 7. EARL & ANITA MAXWELL WITH CAROLYN & TOM GALLAGHER 8. MARIE & BILL AYDAM 9. JOE & SONJA HOLT AT CHILDREN'S HOSPITAL GALA 1997

1

2

3

4

5

6

7

A new event began in this era, the Fine Wine Auction and Dinner benefiting the Austin Symphony. Held at the Four Seasons Hotel, it brought chefs from across town to each prepare a course for a 6-8 course dinner. As no chef wants to fail in front of their peers, the quality and plating of each course tended to the remarkable. Purely as a measure of journalistic thoroughness, I got to sample each course. Lots of highlights, but a black bean soup by David Garrido remains in my memory for 20 years now—an absolutely perfect balance of bean and acid that made each bite as superb as the first one.

8

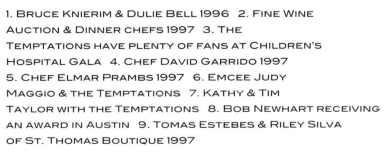

9

1. BRUCE KNIERIM & DULIE BELL 1996   2. FINE WINE AUCTION & DINNER CHEFS 1997   3. THE TEMPTATIONS HAVE PLENTY OF FANS AT CHILDREN'S HOSPITAL GALA   4. CHEF DAVID GARRIDO 1997 5. CHEF ELMAR PRAMBS 1997   6. EMCEE JUDY MAGGIO & THE TEMPTATIONS   7. KATHY & TIM TAYLOR WITH THE TEMPTATIONS   8. BOB NEWHART RECEIVING AN AWARD IN AUSTIN   9. TOMAS ESTEBES & RILEY SILVA OF ST. THOMAS BOUTIQUE 1997

1. LADY BIRD JOHNSON IS HAPPY WITH GOOD NEWS FOR THE WILDFLOWER CENTER   2. WANDA GODWIN & LADY BIRD JOHNSON   3. THE GROUNDBREAKING FOR THE HEART HOSPITAL IN OCTOBER 1997   4. LADY BIRD JOHNSON ON HER 85TH BIRTHDAY   5. GAY RATLIFF, BETH GRANGER & MARY LOU MORRISON   6. PAUL BEUTEL, MARIE CRANE, EDDIE SAFADY & TAM ROGERS   7. DAN & CLAYTON BULLOCK   8. LAMBROS LAMBROU & COOKIE RUIZ OF BALLET AUSTIN IN JUNE 1997

1. CHARLES BARNETT & KELLY WHITE 2. EDEN & HAL BOX
WITH LUCI JOHNSON 3. BEN & MELANIE BARNES AT FINE WINE
AUCTION & DINNER 4. VICKIE & RON KESSLER
5. CHARMAINE & GORDON MCGILL AT PHANTOM OF THE OPERA
GALA CELEBRATING THE RENOVATION OF BASS CONCERT HALL
FEBRUARY 1998 6. GERALD & CINDY STONE 7. RICHARD &
MARTHA COONS WITH PETER BAY 8. CAROL THOMPSON & THE
PHANTOM (HOWARD CHALMERS) 9. JACK & JANET ROBERTS
10. BOBBIE & RENEE GIRLING

1. Jane Sibley, Peter Bay & Joe Long at the signing of Peter Bay's contract with the Austin Symphony Orchestra in February 1998   2. Ms. Thomas with Etta Moore at Rhinestone Campout 1998   3. Sarah & Dick Rathgeber with Roseanna Szilak   4. Nona Niland & Eddie Safady at People's Community Clinic gathering in March 1998   5. Melanie & Ben Barnes   6. The King family gathers   7. Texas Book Festival committee meeting 1998   8. Alfred & Ellen King 1998   9. Stephanie Sobotik, John Aielli & Peggy Hubble

1. MICHELLE JUST-LINDER & TED LINDER   2. GERRY & ROBERT ERSEK   3. LAURA BUSH, DAMIAN PRIOUR & GEORGE BUSH AT ART BALL TWO 1998   4. LAURA & GEORGE BUSH   5. AMOA DIRECTOR ELIZABETH FERRER & GEORGE BUSH   6. SHEILA PAYNTER, VINCE SACK & MEG LOWRY, RON PAYNTER   7. KIRK WATSON, JULIE OLES, MIKE LEVY, DOROTHY DRUMMER & PAT OLES   8. FRIEND, GRACE JONES & FRANK MORRIS   9. HARRY MIDDLETON & LADY BIRD JOHNSON

111

1. Neal Kocurek April 1998   2. Lyric Opera Gala committee 1998   3. Jan Bullock & Elizabeth Christian   4. George Christian, Elizabeth Christian & Jo Anne Christian 5. Jan Bullock, Lady Bird Johnson & friend   6. Nancy & Bob Inman   7. Orange Jackets Gyneth Williams, Sug Danforth & Kim Danforth   8. Joe & Teresa Long with Betty & Bill King

1. Alex Albright, Cyndy Hughes & Mary Margaret Farabee at First Edition Literary Gala 1998   2. Linda & Bill Raman   3. Barbara Blaine, Gary Cartwright, Phyllis Cartwright & Larry L King   4. Gerron & Jessie Otto Hite   5. Laura & George Bush with Jenna Welch   6. Sherri & Winston Krause   7. Billy & Regan Gammon, Cyndy Hughes, Jan & David Hughes   8. Jim Davis, Mary Margaret Farabee & Larry L King   9. Jon & Tina Kemmerer

113

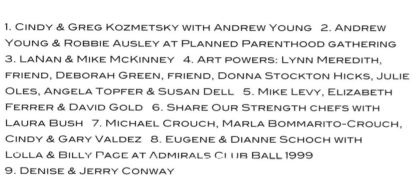

1. Cindy & Greg Kozmetsky with Andrew Young   2. Andrew Young & Robbie Ausley at Planned Parenthood gathering   3. LaNan & Mike McKinney   4. Art powers: Lynn Meredith, friend, Deborah Green, friend, Donna Stockton Hicks, Julie Oles, Angela Topfer & Susan Dell   5. Mike Levy, Elizabeth Ferrer & David Gold   6. Share Our Strength chefs with Laura Bush   7. Michael Crouch, Marla Bommarito-Crouch, Cindy & Gary Valdez   8. Eugene & Dianne Schoch with Lolla & Billy Page at Admirals Club Ball 1999   9. Denise & Jerry Conway

1. JAMES HUFFINES IN RETRO ATTIRE   2. CHER & SONNY, OTHERWISE KNOWN AS NONA NILAND & EDDIE SAFADY   3. MARGARET & FRANK KRASOVEC 4. JULIE & BEN CRENSHAW   5. FRANK & MELISSA JACKSON   6. DONNA STOCKTON HICKS & STEVE HICKS TRAVEL BACK TO DISCO DAYS   NOVEMBER 1998 7. VENUS & BILL STRAWN   8. MARK & BECKY POWELL   9. HELEN BOWDEN, SISTER GERTRUDE LEVY & KAREN KAHAN

1. SHERRY BUCHANAN, JULIE OLES & KAREN OSWALT   2. STEPHEN & DEBORAH YURCO WITH JOAN RIVERS   3. ALAN & MARTHA MOORE WITH JOAN RIVERS   4. SISTER GERTRUDE LEVY & JOAN RIVERS (BEFORE)   5. SISTER GERTRUDE LEVY & JOAN RIVERS (AFTER)   6. JOAN RIVERS WITH ANGELA & MORT TOPFER AT SETON GALA 1999   7. KEVIN BENZ & OLGA CAMPOS AT CHILDREN'S HOSPITAL GALA 1999

1. Sarah Godwin enjoys her modeling moment at Symphony League Fashion Show 1999   2. George & Laura Bush
3. Robert Duvall & George Bush
4. Chris Mattsson with Christopher & Amy Carrier at First Edition Literary Gala 1999   5. Neal & Mary Kocurek
6. Sally Wittliff with Robert Duvall

1. Melanie & Ben Barnes with Jehan Sadat   2. Kaye & Pat Forgione with Jehan Sadat
3. Ben Barnes & Jehan Sadat   4. Mack & Sally Brown at a groundbreaking at Helping
Hand Home   5. Howard & Mary Chalmers with Lance Armstrong   6. Jeff & Bonita
Garvey with Lance Armstrong   7. Sally & Mack Brown with Kay Broline

CHAPTER FIVE 2000–2005

The population of Travis County grew from just over 800,000 to just over 900,000. Rick Perry became governor. Kirk Watson was mayor before Gus Garcia and then Will Wynn.

A few hours before the Harvey Penick Award Dinner honoring Ben Crenshaw in 2001, an absolute monsoon hit Austin. I set out in howling wind and sideways rain for the Four Seasons Hotel with only journalistic pride pushing me on. I managed to get there, but over half the expected crowd simply couldn't get over Bull Creek and Shoal Creek to reach the hotel. Emcee Gary Farmer had the best line of the night when he welcomed everyone to the "first ever all-you-can-eat Harvey Penick Award Dinner."

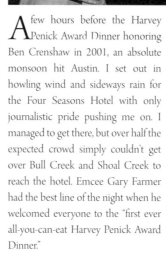

1. Gathered for Harvey Penick Award presentation to Ben Crenshaw 2. Village People performed at the 2000 Children's Hospital Gala 3. A fan meets Lady Bird Johnson 4. Austin Musical Theatre benefit 5. Ben Crenshaw's 50th birthday party 2002 6. Friend, Susan Dell & Julie Crenshaw 7. Bill & Bettye Nowlin 8. Roy & Linda Bush at groundbreaking at Caswell House 2000 9. Kirk Watson, Calvin Trillin & Molly Ivins 10. Gary Farmer & Ben Crenshaw 11. Peggy Pickle meets Calvin Trillin

1. MARK POWELL, MICHAEL DELL & JIM MORITZ 2. MARY BETH ROGERS AT THE 25TH ANNIVERSARY OF AUSTIN CITY LIMITS IN OCTOBER 2000 3. SUSAN DELL & REBECCA HARDEMAN 4. STEVE HICKS, DONNA STOCKTON HICKS, MICHAEL & SUSAN DELL, RICK PERRY 5. FRIENDS OF AUSTIN MUSICAL THEATRE 6. CINDY BUSBY & JULIE SMITH 7. TILTON HUGHES, FRIEND, ROBIN & MALCOLM COOPER 8. JIM & KATHY LOCKART 9. STEPHEN HARRIGAN WITH HIS DAUGHTER AT HOSPICE AUSTIN BENEFIT 10. JULIE SAYERS, ANITA PERRY & PATTY HOFFPAUIR 11. GERRON & JESSIE OTTO HITE WITH CHIP & KAREN OSWALT

121

1. DARRELL ROYAL, WILLIE NELSON & RON FRANKLIN AT 25TH ANNIVERSARY OF AUSTIN CITY LIMITS 2000 2. NEAL KOCUREK & FRIEND 3. FRIEND, VICKI ROAN, SHEILA PAYNTER, TOMI WINSTEAD, BONNIE FRANKLIN 4. BUDDY & GINNY JONES WITH NANCY & NYLE MAXWELL 5. MELANIE & BEN BARNES WITH THEIR PET CHICKEN 6. KILYONG NATHO, SHARON WILSON, SONIA WILSON, NANCY YOUNG & BETTY KING 7. KINKY FRIEDMAN 8. ANITA PERRY & HER SON GRIFFIN AT HOSPICE AUSTIN SENIOR PRESENTATION 2002 9. SAM & KAREN BOATRIGHT WITH CHARLES BAILEY 10.ALEX ALBRIGHT WITH ANNA & SCOTT BAKER

1. Van & Jeanne Hoisington 2. Ronnie Earle, friend & Robert Kennedy, Jr. at Austin Community Foundation event 3. A construction tour of the Long Center 4. Toni & Paul Burns 5. A gathering of men supporting SafePlace 6. Peggy & Michael Frary 7. Gail & Jeff Kodosky 8. Angela Topfer 2002 9. Gene Fondren, Amy Wilson, Deborah & Larry Peel 10. Donna Stockton Hicks, Lance Armstrong, Deborah Green & Anita Perry

1

2

I cover four debutante presentations a year—Bachelors, Helping Hand, Admirals and Symphony. The two in the spring, Bachelors and Helping Hand, have the most with a total of nearly 50 debutantes. Admirals and Symphony in the fall offer about a dozen. Multiply that by 37 years, and I'm somewhere in the 2000-debutantes range. Most delightful shot of all that time came when little Caroline Symcox signaled her approval of Weston Lipscomb and Will Hardeman. Happened in a blink so I was very pleased to have been ready to capture the moment.

3

4

5

6

7

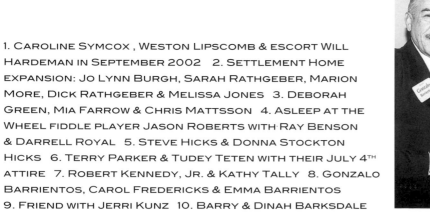

8

9

10

1. CAROLINE SYMCOX , WESTON LIPSCOMB & ESCORT WILL HARDEMAN IN SEPTEMBER 2002   2. SETTLEMENT HOME EXPANSION: JO LYNN BURGH, SARAH RATHGEBER, MARION MORE, DICK RATHGEBER & MELISSA JONES   3. DEBORAH GREEN, MIA FARROW & CHRIS MATTSSON   4. ASLEEP AT THE WHEEL FIDDLE PLAYER JASON ROBERTS WITH RAY BENSON & DARRELL ROYAL   5. STEVE HICKS & DONNA STOCKTON HICKS   6. TERRY PARKER & TUDEY TETEN WITH THEIR JULY 4TH ATTIRE   7. ROBERT KENNEDY, JR. & KATHY TALLY   8. GONZALO BARRIENTOS, CAROL FREDERICKS & EMMA BARRIENTOS 9. FRIEND WITH JERRI KUNZ   10. BARRY & DINAH BARKSDALE

1. CAROL THOMPSON & EDDIE SAFADY AT TERRY FOX DINNER 2. MARY GORDON SPENCE & JUDY MAGGIO 3. EDWARD BUTLER, ANN BUTLER, RENEE BUTLER & ROY BUTLER 4. LISA RODMAN, MARCIA WALLACE & SUZANNE MOORE AT BREAST CANCER RESOURCE CENTER EVENT 5. DAVID & DEALEY HERNDON & FRIEND 6. DONNA STOCKTON HICKS & STEVE HICKS WITH CHILDREN 7. A GATHERING OF SYMPHONY KNIGHTS 8. ANDREW & MARY ANN HELLER WITH STEPHEN STILLS & PETER BAY 9. COURTNEY HOFFMAN & HER FATHER, JULIAN READ 10. JACK & CARLA MCDONALD 11. DEAN & ANDREA MCWILLIAMS

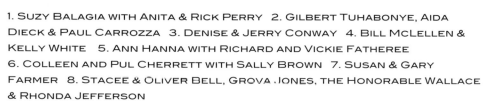

1. Suzy Balagia with Anita & Rick Perry   2. Gilbert Tuhabonye, Aida Dieck & Paul Carrozza   3. Denise & Jerry Conway   4. Bill McLellen & Kelly White   5. Ann Hanna with Richard and Vickie Fatheree   6. Colleen and Pul Cherrett with Sally Brown   7. Susan & Gary Farmer   8. Stacee & Oliver Bell, Grova Jones, the Honorable Wallace & Rhonda Jefferson

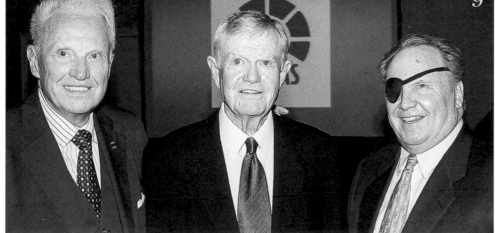

1. Isabella Cunningham, Jody Conradt & DeLoss Dodds 2. Tim & Mary Herman with Richard Slaughter 3. Seton Gala gathering 2003 4. Robbie Ausley & Glenda Parks 5. Bill & Rita Keenan 6. Mary Francis & James Schneider 7. Robin & Bud Shivers Bill & Rita Keenan 8. Mike Levy & Diane Carr 9. Frank Denius, Darrell Royal & Lowell Lebermann

127

1. FILM HALL OF FAME: HORTON FOOTE WITH BILL PAXTON & HIS SON   2. PETER FONDA & EDDIE SAFADY   3. DR. JOE & ARTHUREE QUANDER WITH STEPHEN QUANDER   4. DAWNNA DUKES & AMALIA RODRIGUEZ MENDOZA   5. JAY WATSON, TIM MCCLURE & TURK PIPKIN   6. STUART & ANNE ASHMAN   7. YING MCGUIRE GETTING READY FOR ASIAN LUNAR NEW YEAR GALA   8. LEE WALKER & DARYL SLUSHER   9. TOM & LYNN MEREDITH AT TERRY FOX DINNERTO BENEFIT SHIVERS RADIATION CENTER   10. BOBBIE BARKER, LEE WALKER & RON KESSLER

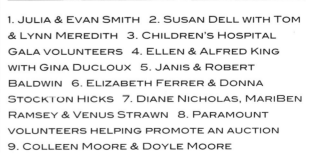

1. JULIA & EVAN SMITH 2. SUSAN DELL WITH TOM & LYNN MEREDITH 3. CHILDREN'S HOSPITAL GALA VOLUNTEERS 4. ELLEN & ALFRED KING WITH GINA DUCLOUX 5. JANIS & ROBERT BALDWIN 6. ELIZABETH FERRER & DONNA STOCKTON HICKS 7. DIANE NICHOLAS, MARIBEN RAMSEY & VENUS STRAWN 8. PARAMOUNT VOLUNTEERS HELPING PROMOTE AN AUCTION 9. COLLEEN MOORE & DOYLE MOORE

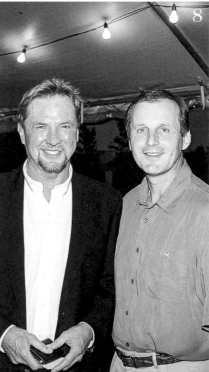

1. RON & SHEILA PAYNTER WITH MEG LOWRY & VINCE SACKS
2. BETH SMITH & BETH PLATER   3. WENDY & SHANNON
KRATZER   4. DONNA STOCKTON HICKS & STEVE HICKS
5. PARAMOUNT GALA WITH PATTI LUPONE   6. RONYA
KOZMETSKY & CINDY KOZMETSKY   7. SUSAN & MICHAEL DELL
8. GREG HURD & RICK BARNES   9. PEGGY HUBBLE & DONNA
BALDWIN   10. KAREN & SAM BOATRIGHT

1. Sarah Butler & Karen Johnson   2. Bobbi & Mort Topfer
3. Pam & George Willeford with Ann & Layton Wilson   4. Vicki
& Jim Rado   5. Norm & Julie Smith   6. Ray Benson & Kelly White
7. Liz & Mike Maples   8. Deborah Green & Clayton Aynesworth
9. Richard Byron, Patti LuPone & Scott Thompson

1. Fine Wine Auction & Dinner committee 2. Art Ball 2000
3. Clare & Rick Lotspeich 4. Susan McDowell awards
Blain & Alexa Wesner an "Oscar" from LifeWorks
5. Lesley Varghese with Doug & Margaret Danforth
6. Judy & John Avery at Ronald McDonald House
7. David & Sylvia Jabour 8. Pam & Rick Whitley

132

1. Karen Landa & Peter Bay   2. Sue & Aubrey Smith   3. Leslie & Karl Holtzman with John Cullen & friend   4. Cindy Greenwood, Martina McBride & Suann Waight   5. M P Mueller & Susan McDowell 6. Frank & Nina Seely & friends   7. Dedication of the Neal Kocurek Health Science Institute February 2005   8. Ginger & Jack Blanton 9. Lynn Remadna & Jenna McEachern

1. Asian Lunar New Year Gala committee & guests   2. Will Wynn, Joe Pantoliano & Matt Curtis   3. Stacy & Chad Auler   4. Susan Dell dresses at Art Ball 2000   5. Richard Byron, Paul Beutel & Steve Thompson   6. Nicole Covert & Luci Johnson   7. Julie & John Thornton   8. Steve & Ava Late   9. Donaji Lira & Lance Avery Morgan

1. KENT LANCE, REBECCA ROBINSON & MICHAEL VILIM   2. TERESA & JOE LONG ARRIVE FOR THE CULTURE OF ARTS AWARDS   3. ROBERT BERNSTEIN & JOAN LAVA   4. MICHAEL & SUSAN DELL WITH DEBORAH & TOM GREEN & DAUGHTER   5. LESLIE SWEET & JILL REYNOLDS OF HEB PRESENT A CHECK TO DR. JUANITA ORNELAS   6. GAYLE & JIM CULLINGTON   7. LOUISE & PETER PINCOFFS   8. EDDIE SAFADY WITH MELANIE & BEN BARNES   9. CACTUS & PEGGY PRYOR WITH ROBERT BERNSTEIN   10. COLLEEN & DICK HARDIN

1. Kirk Watson, Bruce Malone, Carl Stuart & Joe Annis
2. Shannon & Gay Ratliff with Vicki Roan   3. Ben Barnes being "arrested" for a good cause—a benefit for People's Community Clinic   4. Friend, Robert Bernstein, Elspeth & Walt Rostow   5. Bob & Ann Huthnance
6. Richard & Martha Coons with June & Mark Chandler
7. Neal & Mary Kocurek   8. Cathy & Joe Powell with Missy & N D Moscoe

1. LINDA BALL & FORREST PREECE 2. MARTHA & CARROLL MCPHERSON 3. AL & MARY ANN GOLDEN 4. HONOREES AT THE 6TH ANNUAL LIFEWORKS ACADEMY AWARDS GALA IN MARCH 2000 5. BETTY HIMMELBLAU & JOAN HOLTZMAN 6. LADY BIRD JOHNSON & DJ SIBLEY (ELLEN CARTER & FRIEND IN BACKGROUND) 7. STEVE LEEKE & LORI LEEKE WITH KAREN & PAUL LEEKE 8. MONIQUE & ROBERT THOMAJAN AT FINE WINE AUCTION & DINNER 2000 9. LAEL & GEORGE SEAGERT

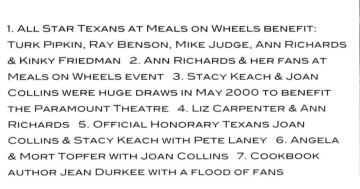

1. All Star Texans at Meals on Wheels benefit: Turk Pipkin, Ray Benson, Mike Judge, Ann Richards & Kinky Friedman   2. Ann Richards & her fans at Meals on Wheels event   3. Stacy Keach & Joan Collins were huge draws in May 2000 to benefit the Paramount Theatre   4. Liz Carpenter & Ann Richards   5. Official Honorary Texans Joan Collins & Stacy Keach with Pete Laney   6. Angela & Mort Topfer with Joan Collins   7. Cookbook author Jean Durkee with a flood of fans

1. AUSTIN MUSICAL THEATRE GATHERING WITH SCOTT THOMPSON, MARY CHALMERS, SUZANNE WINKELMAN, RICHARD BYRON & CINDY HOLCOMB 2. JEAN DURKEE & FRIEND SHOW OFF RECIPE RESULT
3. DEBORAH GREEN & JOAN COLLINS 4. JOAN COLLINS & EVENT HOST CHARLES DUGGAN 5. JOAN COLLINS & RON KNIGHT 6. DONNA STOCKTON HICKS & JOAN COLLINS
7. RAY BENSON'S FANS COME IN ALL SIZES—LIKE LITTLE SARAH GODWIN 8. ELIZABETH CHRISTIAN & BRUCE TODD WITH JOAN COLLINS 9. PEGGY HUBBLE & BRUCE TODD SHARE A LAUGH WITH STACY KEACH

139

1. JOE & PEGGY ANNIS WITH JOAN LAVA & FRIEND   2. UNITED WAY GROUP WITH JOY LEGAN (RIGHT)   3. STEPHEN & DEBORAH YURCO LISTENING TO JEFF GARVEY   4. AUBREY & SUE SMITH WITH FRIENDS   5. DON COOK, PEGGY PICKLE, SAM & SONIA WILSON, KATHY & PHIL PATMAN   6. STEVE PAPERMASTER SHOWS OFF SURPRISING STRENGTH   7. CLAY MCPHAIL FAMILY WITH LARRY GATLIN   8. CLIFF & CHRIS COLLIER WITH SCOTT THOMPSON

1. MARY ANN & ANDREW HELLER 2. KEITH & LOUISE CROWLEY 3. ROGER & MARY ELLEN BORGELT WITH LINDA & ROY BUSH 4. MIKE LEVY, TURK PIPKIN, STEVE PAPERMASTER & KIRK WATSON AT JUVENILE DIABETES EVENT 5. RAY & JENNENE MASHBURN, DIANE CARR, RAY BENSON, FRIEND, BECKY & RICHARD HERRINGTON FOR BALLET AUSTIN 6. RICHARD BYRON & SCOTT THOMPSON OF AUSTIN MUSICAL THEATRE 7. SETON VOLUNTEERS WITH SISTER GERTRUDE LEVY 8. JOE & BECKY WORKMAN WITH ED & BIRDIE KUEMPEL 9. PHILIP BRELAND, BILLY MEYERS & CATHY POWELL

141

1. FRIEND, STEPHEN MILLS & NINA SEELY   2. JAN
HUGHES, FRIEND, JO ANNE CHRISTIAN & JAN BULLOCK
3. UNITED WAY REP WITH MORT & ANGELA TOPFER
4. DEBORAH & TOM GREEN WITH MARY BETH ROGERS
5. LIZ CARPENTER & LIZ SMITH   6. GREG & CINDY
KOZMETSKY AT CHILDREN'S HOSPITAL   7. LIZ WATSON
& AMY DAVIDSON

1. Pris & Peter Flawn   2. Peggy & Ron Weiss   3. Sen. John & Sandy Cornyn   4. Bill & Ann Norman with Jean & David Murph   5. John Kelso & book fans at Austin Country Club   6. Amanda Beck, Liz Smith & Julie Crenshaw 7. George Plimpton, Elizabeth Christian, Bruce Todd, Peggy & Cactus Pryor at First Edition Literary Gala 2000   8. Ann Richards & Bud Shrake

1. Rick Perry goes airborne for United Way 2. Mary Beth Kiser, Diane Taaffe & Christi Cox 3. Ann Richards, Ellen Richards & Mary Pipher 4. Bettie & Bob Girling with Carole McClellan 5. Alan & Susan Sager with Karl Rove 6. Melanie Fish, Terry Quinn & Susan Sealy 7. Karen Cox & friends at United Way gathering January 2000 8. Pat Hayes & friend

1. JOE & TERESA LONG WITH KARL ROVE
2. NATIONAL CHARITY LEAGUE GATHERING
3. PETE & TOMI WINSTEAD WITH JEANNE &
LEW LITTLE   4. ANN COULTER IN ANIMATED
CONVERSATION WHILE AUSTIN BAY LOOKS
FOR SHELTER   5. NATIONAL CHARITY LEAGUE
GATHERING   6. NATIONAL CHARITY LEAGUE
GATHERING   7. ANN COULTER PROMOTES HER
BOOK   8. KARL ROVE WITH PAT & JULIE OLES

1. Rita Coolidge with Ed & Susan Auler at Seton Gala October 2000
2. Susan Dell applauded for her design work 3. Diane, Howard & Nicole Falkenberg at Fine Art Festival 4. Paul Cherrett with Tom & Deborah Green 5. Alzheimer's Research support committee gathering April 2001
6. Karen Oswalt, Aimee Laughlin & Deborah Green 7. Susan Dell & Karen Cox of CASA 8. Charlotte & Weston Lipscomb

1. Susan Dell & Margaret Krasovec
2. Elizabeth Ferrer explains a possible museum plan to Tom Meredith   3. Toast of the Town party April 2001   4. Becky Beaver & friend Women's Fund luncheon May 2001   5. Rita Coolidge with Bob & Ann Huthnance   6. Women's Fund luncheon May 2001   7. Rita Coolidge with Sister Gertrude Levy   8. Mike Kelly interviews Madeleine Albright   9. Kendra Scott & Claudia Tejeda

1. UNITED WAY TOTAL JANUARY 2000
2. ASSISTANCE LEAGUE GATHERING 3. RITA &
MATT KREISLE 4. WOMEN OF DISTINCTION 2001
5. BILL COSBY RELAXING WITH ANGELA TOPFER
& SUSAN DELL 6. MORT & ANGELA TOPFER WITH
BILL COSBY 7. ANGELA TOPFER & SUSAN DELL
8. JOHN & MARGARET MOSS OF SWEETBRUSH
9. ELIZABETH CHRISTIAN & BILL HOBBY

148

1. Jake Pickle & his famous 4th of July tie
2. Friend with Carl Stuart & Claire Stuart at People's Community Clinic event 3. Jake & Beryl Pickle 4. E A Seton "Evening Under the Stars" committee meeting September 2001
5. Liz Carpenter, Rick Hardin & Lady Bird Johnson 6. The Beck family meets Rita Coolidge 7. Mary Margaret & Ray Farabee with Sue McBee 8. Seton Gala Co-Chair Ann Honeycutt, Harry Conick, Sr. & Gala Co-Chair Amy Ehrlich 9. Ballet Austin Guild gathering

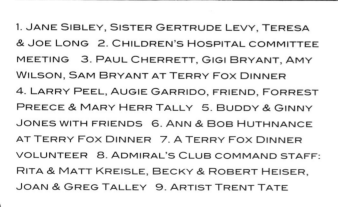

1. Jane Sibley, Sister Gertrude Levy, Teresa & Joe Long 2. Children's Hospital committee meeting 3. Paul Cherrett, Gigi Bryant, Amy Wilson, Sam Bryant at Terry Fox Dinner 4. Larry Peel, Augie Garrido, friend, Forrest Preece & Mary Herr Tally 5. Buddy & Ginny Jones with friends 6. Ann & Bob Huthnance at Terry Fox Dinner 7. A Terry Fox Dinner volunteer 8. Admiral's Club command staff: Rita & Matt Kreisle, Becky & Robert Heiser, Joan & Greg Talley 9. Artist Trent Tate

CHAPTER SIX 2006-2012

The population of Travis County continues to grow from just over 900,000 to over 1,000,000. Rick Perry continues as governor. Will Wynn was mayor until Lee Leffingwell took over in 2009. A new addition to the gala benefits was Dancing with the Stars Austin, benefiting the Center for Child Protection. Local celebrities are paired with professional dancers with outstanding entertainment results for the attending crowd.

1. George & Ann Attal with Bobbi & Mort Topfer for March of Dimes 2. Nancy Merritt & Amanda Beck 3. Mary Elizabeth Gray with her father, Jeff Gray 2006 4. Chris Peele, Monica Pottorff & Any Baby Can award 5. Patty & James Huffines 6. Audie Walker helps Bachelors Club debutantes

1. Richard Slaughter (second from left) & Austin Community Foundation 2. Friend with Mr. & Mrs. David Hilgers 3. Liz Carpenter with Reuben Johnson & Harry Middleton 2006 4. Jeanne & Rusty Parker with Ava Late 5. Faith in Action gathering 2006 6. Julie Oles with Mike & LaNan McKinney 7. Cord & Anne Shiflet 8. Kate & Robert Hersch at ArtHouse 2006 9. Mr. & Mrs. Bechtol

1. DR. THOMAS & KAREN VAUGHN 2. TINA & JON KEMMERER 3. CINDY KOZMETSKY, RONYA KOZMETSKY & GREG KOZMETSKY 4. CHRISTI & GUS GONZALES 5. KAYE & PAT FORGIONE WITH MICHELLE GODWIN 6. PETER STAATS & ANN FORMAN 2006 7. MARY ANN & ANDREW HELLER 8. GEORGE & ANN ATTAL 9. JOANNA & BRENT WEBER

1. JIM STONE & KENT LANCE 2. KARL ROVE & BEN BENTZIN
3. CAROLYN GALLAGHER WITH BRIAN & JANE GREIG
4. FRIENDS WITH CHEF CHARLES MAYES (SECOND FROM LEFT)
5. LAURIE & FRANKLIN HALL 6. DOROTHY & CHARLES NASH
7. ALAN SAGER, DEBORAH PEEL, SUSAN SAGER, SUSAN
COMBS & LARRY PEEL 8. LYLE LOVETT

1. James Armstrong, Marjorie Mulanax, Larry Connelly & Karen Landa   2. Jane & Michael Driscoll   3. Getting ready for A Christmas Affair with Beth Smith (right)
4. Pat & Julie Oles   5. Fun shopping with: friend Sally Brown, friend, Andrea McWilliams, friend   6. Jim & Vicki Rado   7. Mary Ann & Randy Maltz   8. Lynn & Tom Meredith
9. Cindy & Greg Kozmetsky

1. LINKS MARDI GRAS PARTY WITH MACHREE GIBSON, STACEE BELL & BRENDA KELLEY   2. CECILIA & GREG ABBOTT WITH HEIDI & TED CRUZ   3. HARVEY & MICHELE KRONBERG WITH HELEN & ED BAXTER   4. REGAN GAMMON & FRIEND   5. LINKS MARDI GRAS PARTY: SHERI JACKSON & LAMONICA LEWIS   6. BILL & SALLY WITTLIFF   7. LEE THOMSON, MARK STRAMA, CLARKE HEIDRICK, & FRIEND   8. RUSTY TALLY, JEANNE PARKER, EVA & MARVIN WOMACK, GLORIA EVANS   9. MR. & MRS. TREY HALBERT

1. Ruth Kohlhaas, Tomi Winstead & Vicki Roan 2. Dan & Darlene Byrne 3. David Chan, James Lee & Lucia Hur at Asian Lunar New Year Gala 4. Gangs all here, for Lyric Opera 5. Music Miracles at St. Andrew's School with Joe McDermott 6. Vicki Roan & Cliff Redd 7. Bettye Nowlin, Regina Rogoff & Joan Lava 8. Sandy Dorf & Karen Landa

1. Scarlett Lewis & Nina Seely   2. Chris Mattsson, Deborah Green & Bettye Nowlin   3. Kent Burress, Carol Crowley, Tomi Winstead & Kenny Jastrow show image of new Ronald McDonald House   4. Carol & Tim Crowley   5. Harris & Emily Baker   6. Sara Fox & Anne Elizabeth Wynn   7. Mort & Bobbi Topfer, Eddie Safady, Ann Richards & Bud Shrake   8. Richard & Rae Hill at Star of Texas Rodeo Gala   9. Wallace & Lanette Smith

159

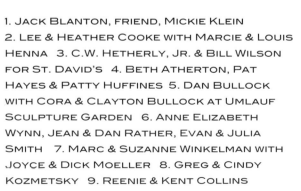

1. Jack Blanton, friend, Mickie Klein
2. Lee & Heather Cooke with Marcie & Louis Henna   3. C.W. Hetherly, Jr. & Bill Wilson for St. David's   4. Beth Atherton, Pat Hayes & Patty Huffines   5. Dan Bullock with Cora & Clayton Bullock at Umlauf Sculpture Garden   6. Anne Elizabeth Wynn, Jean & Dan Rather, Evan & Julia Smith   7. Marc & Suzanne Winkelman with Joyce & Dick Moeller   8. Greg & Cindy Kozmetsky   9. Reenie & Kent Collins

1. Bobby & Jan Jenkins 2. Deborah Green & Jane Schweppe 3. Carol Martin & Janet Tysdal 4. Bill & Bettye Nowlin, Carol & Pat Robertson, Cookie Ruiz 5. Pat Melliar-Smith, Nancy Payne & Stephanie Whitehurst for Assistance League 6. Pat Oles, Gigi & Sam Bryant, Julie Oles & Pam Willeford 7. Nancy Payne, Thelma Price & Peggy Davis for Assistance League 8. Peter Schram & Harry Ullmann for Ballet Austin 9. Lynn & Mary Scott Nabers

1. BEN & MELANIE BARNES WITH STEPHEN MILLS
2. BILL CLEMENTS AT BULLOCK MUSEUM 3. TOM CRADDICK & BILL
CLEMENTS 4. JUDY MAGGIO & THAD ROSENFELD 5. BETH ATHERTON,
ROY MINTON & JO ANNE CHRISTIAN 6. LANAN & MIKE MCKINNEY
7. JAN BULLOCK & BILL CLEMENTS 8. LOWELL LEBERMANN &
SUE MELLER 9. KIRK WATSON, RANDALL'S REPRESENTATIVE, ALICE
WILSON, THAD ROSENFELD FOR BREAST CANCER RESOURCE CENTER

1. KIRK & LIZ WATSON   2. DONNA STOCKTON HICKS & STEVE HICKS   3. DARRELL ROYAL & STEVE HICKS   4. CISSY COOPER WITH MALCOLM & ROBIN COOPER   5. JUDGE JEANNE MEURER & JUDGE RHONDA HURLEY   6. CRAIG HELLA JOHNSON & DAN BULLOCK   7. CASABLANCA IN 2007: BETH & FRANK STABILE   8. JANE DRISCOLL, SUSAN HACKNEY & DONAJI LIRA   9. SARAH GROOS, LEE THOMSON, ANDREA RADO, DAVID ESCAMILLA & ANNE NASH FOR EMERGE AUSTIN 10. RICHARD SLAUGHTER & BRENDA KLEIN

1. GREG & CECILIA ABBOTT WITH THEIR DAUGHTER, AUDREY 2. KAREN & PAUL LEEKE 3. THE RACE IS ON AT THE ANNUAL INHERIT AUSTIN EASTER EGG HUNT 4. CECILIA ABBOTT, JEANNE PARKER & AVA LATE 5. JANIS & JOE PINNELLI 6. JASON EARLE WITH MARGARET JABOUR & DAVID JABOUR 7. DR. JOE & PEGGY ANNIS 8. ETTA MOORE & DAVID ADAIR 9. LARRY CONNELLY, CARLA MCDONALD & JAMES ARMSTRONG 10. ROY RUSHING & MARJORIE MULANAX

1. INHERIT AUSTIN FUN AHEAD 2. ADA ANDERSON & FRIEND
3. ELMER & ANN KELTON, ELIZABETH CROOK & MARC LEWIS,
BARBARA PORTER 4. MARY & TIM HERMAN 5. BARBARA
KOOYMAN, RAY BENSON & MICHELLE VALLES 6. INHERIT
AUSTIN APRIL 2007 7. JAN HUGHES & JAN DEMETRI AT FIRST
EDITION LITERARY GALA 2007 8. EDDIE SAFADY, SUZANNE &
MARC WINKELMAN & DEBORAH PEEL

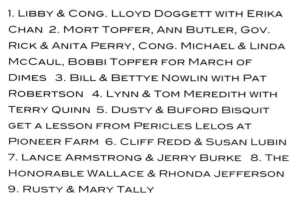

1. Libby & Cong. Lloyd Doggett with Erika Chan 2. Mort Topfer, Ann Butler, Gov. Rick & Anita Perry, Cong. Michael & Linda McCaul, Bobbi Topfer for March of Dimes 3. Bill & Bettye Nowlin with Pat Robertson 4. Lynn & Tom Meredith with Terry Quinn 5. Dusty & Buford Bisquit get a lesson from Pericles Lelos at Pioneer Farm 6. Cliff Redd & Susan Lubin 7. Lance Armstrong & Jerry Burke 8. The Honorable Wallace & Rhonda Jefferson 9. Rusty & Mary Tally

1. BILL JONES—DANCING WITH THE STARS AUSTIN CHAMPION 2007   2. MARIEL HEMINGWAY WITH SUSAN SAGER   3. ANDREA & DEAN MCWILLIAMS   4. KATHY & RANDY TAYLOR   5. MIKE HANLEY, HOWARD CHALMERS, GENE FONDREN & DOYLE FELLERS—KINGS OF THE AUCTION
6. CHARMAINE MCGILL—DANCING WITH THE STARS AUSTIN CHAMPION 2010   7. WENDY KRATZER & MAURINE KOCUREK   8. KAREN KUYKENDALL   9. VAUGHN BROCK—DANCING WITH THE STARS AUSTIN CHAMPION 2011

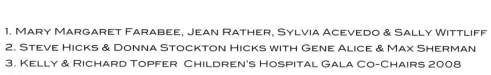

1. Mary Margaret Farabee, Jean Rather, Sylvia Acevedo & Sally Wittliff
2. Steve Hicks & Donna Stockton Hicks with Gene Alice & Max Sherman
3. Kelly & Richard Topfer Children's Hospital Gala Co-Chairs 2008
4. Beth Atherton with Sally & Mack Brown 5. Carla McDonald, Kate Hersch & Julie Thornton 6. Dave Steakley—Dancing with the Stars Austin Champion 2009 7. Eric & Maria Groten 8. Ray & Jennene Mashburn 9. Lowell Lebermann & Lee Walker

1. RONDA GRAY—DANCING WITH THE STARS AUSTIN CHAMPION 2008 2. ANDRA LIEMANDT—DANCING WITH THE STARS AUSTIN CHAMPION 2012 3. GRETCHEN BARBER, JOHN PAUL DEJORIA, BILLY GIBBONS, ELOISE DEJORIA, LEA BUFFINGTON 4. SHARON SCHWEITZER ROBINSON & JOHN ROBINSON 5. KRISTY OZMUN & MANDY DEALEY 6. ANN & ROY BUTLER 7. WILHELMINA & EXALTON DELCO WITH KERRY TATE 8. PATTI & JIM STONE

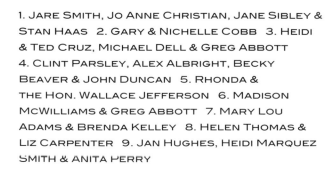

1. Jare Smith, Jo Anne Christian, Jane Sibley & Stan Haas 2. Gary & Nichelle Cobb 3. Heidi & Ted Cruz, Michael Dell & Greg Abbott 4. Clint Parsley, Alex Albright, Becky Beaver & John Duncan 5. Rhonda & the Hon. Wallace Jefferson 6. Madison McWilliams & Greg Abbott 7. Mary Lou Adams & Brenda Kelley 8. Helen Thomas & Liz Carpenter 9. Jan Hughes, Heidi Marquez Smith & Anita Perry

1. Rick & Karen Hawkins 2. Randy & Kathy Taylor with Forest Roan for Lung Association 3. Michael & Susan Dell with Lynn & Tom Meredith 4. Kay & Bobby Gregory 5. Willie Nelson 2008 6. Turk Pipkin & Dick Clark 7. Harry Ullmann & Peter Schram 8. Mary Margaret Farabee & Bettye Nowlin

1. JASON & ANNA HERD WITH ROBERT EARL KEEN AT E A SETON
PICNIC UNDER THE STARS 2. TANYA & POLICE CHIEF ART ACEVEDO
3. CELEBRATING TOAST OF THE TOWN'S 25TH ANNIVERSARY 4. IF
ONLY AL GOLDEN COULD GET ENTHUSIASTIC AS A SPOTTER FOR THE
RARE WINE AUCTION 5. JOSE BUITRON, BILL PITTS, CYNDI & BILL
BOCK 6. MANOT & FOO SWASDEE 7. RONDA & KELLY GRAY
8. JERRY & DENISE CONWAY

1. Olga Campos & Cookie Ruiz   2. Will Wynn & Lee Thomson
3. Jack & Ginger Blanton   4. Kirk Watson, Will Wynn & Roy Butler
5. Walter Cronkite & Julie Oles   6. Rudy Green & Joyce Christian
7. Laura Wolf (CASA) & Judge Jeanne Meurer   8. June & Mark
Chandler   9. Becky & Mark Powell   10. Nancy & Nyle Maxwell
11. Herb Kelleher   12. Mentors for I Live Here, I Give Here

173

1. Robert Rodriguez   2. Frank & Beth Stabile   3. Gretchen Barber, John Paul DeJoria, Billy Gibbons, Eloise DeJoria   4. Tito & Lori Beveridge   5. Michael Crouch & Marla Bommarito Crouch   6. Cindy & Gary Valdez   7. Duane & Meredith Cooper   8. Bobby & Jan Jenkins

1. BETH STABILE, LISA PARRISH, MARTHA JENKINS, CYNDI BOCK & MONA CANNON 2. LEE WALKER, JENNIFER VICKERS, ROBIN RATHER, DAN & JEAN RATHER 3. PENNY & DR. THOMAS CEDEL WITH MARY ANN & ROGER STAUBACH AT CONCORDIA EVENT 2007 4. PAM, MALLORY & ALLISON MALONE WITH PATTY DUKE FOR NEW MILESTONES 5. AMY WONG MOK, ADA ANDERSON & ALOYSIUS MOK 6. TOM GILILAND, SYLVIA OROZCO, GRISEL RODRIGUEZ, CHEF MIGUEL RAVAGO FOR MEXIC-ARTE EVENT 7. GAIL & JEFF KODOSKY 8. SAMIA & JOHN JOSEPH 9. ADM. BOB & NANCY INMAN OPENING OF THE LONG CENTER MARCH 2008

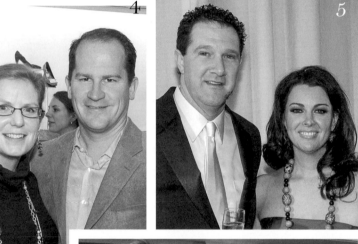

1. VENUS STRAWN, VIOLET BELL, LINDA MCCAUL, STACEE BELL & ANN ATTAL
2. BUD SHRAKE, HARRY ANDERSON, WILLIE NELSON, TURK PIPKIN & OWEN
WILSON 3. ELOISE & JOHN PAUL DEJORIA WITH WILLIE NELSON & FRIEND
4. KAY & ERIC MORELAND 5. KYLE & MONICA BURCHAM 6. PAM & MIKE REESE
FOR NATURE CONSERVANCY 7. MARIEL HEMINGWAY WITH EVENT CHAIRS
JANNA & MITCH JACOBSON FOR NEW MILESTONES 8. CHEF TYSON COLE &
FRIEND FOR MARCH OF DIMES

1. Clary & Dr. Mark Auler 2. Laura Bush & Regan Gammon 3. Lyle Lovett, Sam Shepard, Bill Wittliff, Tommy Lee Jones, Jerry Jeff Walker, Bud Shrake Seated: John Graves for Wittliff Gallery 2006 4. Dan Bullock & Karen Kuykendall 5. Scarlett & John Lewis 6. Nolen Ryan & Dr. Charles Graham 7. Ted & Heidi Cruz with Kristy & Brad Knippa 8. Victoria Avila, David Garza & Sofia Avila 9. Wendy Kratzer & Dinah Street 10. Stacee & Oliver Bell

177

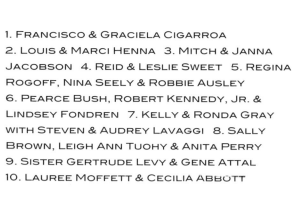

1. Francisco & Graciela Cigarroa
2. Louis & Marci Henna 3. Mitch & Janna Jacobson 4. Reid & Leslie Sweet 5. Regina Rogoff, Nina Seely & Robbie Ausley
6. Pearce Bush, Robert Kennedy, Jr. & Lindsey Fondren 7. Kelly & Ronda Gray with Steven & Audrey Lavaggi 8. Sally Brown, Leigh Ann Tuohy & Anita Perry
9. Sister Gertrude Levy & Gene Attal
10. Lauree Moffett & Cecilia Abbott

1. KEVIN WILLIAMSON & ANTONIO VIDEL OF RANCH 616 FOR LA DOLCE VITA 2009 2. MELISSA JACKSON, DONNA STOCKTON HICKS & PATSY WOODS MARTIN FOR WOMEN'S FUND 3. AUSTIN COUNTRY CLUB WOMEN'S ASSOCIATION bridal memories SHOW 4. ALEX WINKELMAN & SUZANNE WINKELMAN 5. DAMIAN PRIOUR FOR UMLAUF SCULPTURE GARDEN 2009 6. RANDY & DEB GROVES 7. SAM & TIM McCLURE 8. NOLEN & RUTH RYAN FOR HOPE ALLIANCE 9. DAVID JABOUR, DANNY DEVITO & MARGARET JABOUR 10. STEVE HICKS & DONNA STOCKTON HICKS WITH SALLY & MACK BROWN FOR RISE SCHOOL

179

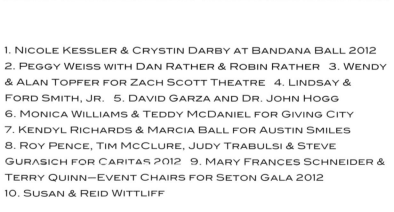

1. Nicole Kessler & Crystin Darby at Bandana Ball 2012
2. Peggy Weiss with Dan Rather & Robin Rather   3. Wendy & Alan Topfer for Zach Scott Theatre   4. Lindsay & Ford Smith, Jr.   5. David Garza and Dr. John Hogg
6. Monica Williams & Teddy McDaniel for Giving City
7. Kendyl Richards & Marcia Ball for Austin Smiles
8. Roy Pence, Tim McClure, Judy Trabulsi & Steve Gurasich for Caritas 2012   9. Mary Frances Schneider & Terry Quinn—Event Chairs for Seton Gala 2012
10. Susan & Reid Wittliff

THE GEORGIA B. LUCAS FOUNDATION FUND OF THE AUSTIN COMMUNITY FOUNDATION

Georgia B. Lucas, daughter of George and Addie Lucas, was born in the historic Warner-Lucas House located at 303 Academy in South Austin and was a lifetime resident of Austin. Before Miss Lucas passed away, she thought to establish the Georgia B. Lucas Foundation Fund of the Austin Community Foundation within her Last Will and Testament.

Thanks to her generosity and forethought, Georgia B. Lucas left a powerful legacy that continues to make a positive impact on our entire community. At its inception, over 15 years ago, the Fund was valued at $5 million. Today, the Fund is valued at nearly $17 million and more than $10 million has been granted to 200 non-profits in Central Texas.

The Georgia B. Lucas Foundation Fund's primary purpose is to provide grants made in the Austin area for several purposes. The first is to provide consistent income on an annual basis to St. David's Hospital, the Salvation Army, Capitol Area Council of Boy Scouts of America, and the Lone Star Girl Scout Council. The balance of the annual income is to be distributed to provide funding in the Central Texas area for groups supporting activities such as the arts and drama, music, historic preservation, youth services, and animal care and protection.

Waterloo Press of the Austin History Center Association gratefully acknowledges the significant contribution of the Georgia B. Lucas Foundation Fund toward the publication of this book. The Austin Community Foundation supports in numerous ways the work of the organizations depicted herein and plays a leading role in making Austin the vital philanthropic community it has been and continues to be.

ACKNOWLEDGMENTS

A complete and thorough acknowledgement of all who helped in the creation of this book would be an entire book itself. Although I have compiled this book, it was written by the people whose faces fill the following pages. It was in chronicling their work over the past 37 years (and counting) that I gathered the material presented here.

I might never have entered the photojournalism world had not my brother, Jay Godwin, found me some photographic odds and ends to do at the *Austin Citizen*. He led the way.

I must thank my colleagues at the *Austin Citizen* for taking in a woefully unqualified photographer and turning him into a photojournalist. I was blessed to have the world's best editor, Carol Fowler, as my first boss. Her black and white definition of professional and work ethics have guided me throughout my career. I was equally blessed to work with Carolyn Bengtson, an extraordinary woman who taught me how the social/charity scene worked in Austin. These two women got me started.

I and the entire community owe quite a debt to Bart Stephens, publisher of the *West Austin News*. For 24 years he provided me personally with a venue for the major portion of my work. For the community at large, he gave a voice to countless non-profits—and continues to do so to this day. It is simply impossible to quantify the amount of work and effort he has put in over the years to keep the paper informing the community of ongoing philanthropic activity.

For this particular bit of work—this book—I need to thank all my friends on Facebook for their encouragement and help in filling in missing names; Lisa Trahan at the St. David's Foundation for general brilliance; Ann Kasper at Saks Fifth Avenue for jump-starting my "I think" to "I will put together a book"; and Kathleen Davis Niendorff of Waterloo Press for embracing the idea. A special thanks must go to the staff of the Austin History Center for their help in navigating the resources of the Center. The talent and tenacity of Terry Sherrell and George Anne Byfield of OneTouchPoint-Ginny's in the design and production of this book have been invaluable, period.

While wholehearted attempts were made to identify every "face" in this book, the constraints of time and memory sometimes prevailed.

Lastly, my wife Michelle has been telling me to create a book since shortly after we started dating. Her acceptance of my very odd schedule is the mark of a special lady. During the work of putting together the book, she reminded me to eat and displayed extraordinary patience when the haz-mat zone known as my office spilled over into the living room.

Robert Godwin

Index

Symbols